The Sharpened Sword

The Sharpened Sword

John Knox

Catherine Mackenzie

CF4•K

10 9 8 7 6 5 4 3 2 1

© Copyright 2012 Catherine Mackenzie

Paperback ISBN: 978-1-78191-057-3

epub ISBN: 978-1-78191-174-7

mobi ISBN: 978-1-78191-175-4

Published by
Christian Focus Publications,
Geanies House, Fearn, Ross-shire,
IV20 1TW, Scotland, U.K.
www.christianfocus.com
e-mail: info@christianfocus.com

Cover design by Daniel van Straaten
Cover illustration by Brent Donahoe
Printed and bound by Nørhaven, Denmark

Scripture quotations are based on the King James Version
of the Bible.

This book is based on the life of John Knox. There is fictional dialogue, but many of the words used by Knox and other key characters are based on what they actually said or wrote. Information was largely taken from Knox's own *History of the Reformation* and Elizabeth Whiteley's *The Plain Mr. Knox*. Information regarding the French galley ship was obtained from an article published by Christian History: Life as a Galley Slave.

Contents

Ephesians 6: 10-18

Finally, my brethren, be strong in the Lord, and in the power of his might.

Put on the whole armour of God, that ye may be able to stand against the wiles of the devil. For we wrestle not against flesh and blood, but against principalities, against powers, against the rulers of the darkness of this world, against spiritual wickedness in high places.

Wherefore take unto you the whole armour of God, that ye may be able to withstand in the evil day, and having done all, to stand.

Stand therefore, having your loins girt about with truth, and having on the breastplate of righteousness;

And your feet shod with the preparation of the gospel of peace; Above all, taking the shield of faith, wherewith ye shall be able to quench all the fiery darts of the wicked. And take the helmet of salvation, and the sword of the Spirit, which is the word of God: Praying always with all prayer and supplication in the Spirit, and watching thereunto with all perseverance and supplication for all saints.

Written with thanks to Almighty God for the impact of his Word on my life. The Sword of the Spirit; the Word made flesh, wielded by many men and women, family and friends in order to bring me to faith. May the children's children carry the same sword to the same effect on future generations.

What's in the News?

If a pile of newspapers was spread in front of you on a table, what articles would you read first? If they had all been printed in the year of your birth, what stories and headlines would grab your attention?

It's possible that there was an election that year or perhaps a major law was passed by the government. Perhaps a film star got married. Was there a war on or a serious international incident in the year of your birth?

Well, if exciting stories happened during the year you were born, they definitely happened in the year 1513, because that year was at the beginning of a breathtaking time in history. The 1500s were full of intrigue. It was an era of danger and discovery. It was a time when real change was happening throughout Europe … and the world.

It hadn't been that long since Christopher Columbus had discovered America. Before that, people had said that there was nothing but sea off the West Coast of Ireland. However, when Columbus set off in a ship and discovered new lands, new animals and new people, the sceptics were proved wrong.

It wasn't just new countries that were being discovered in the 1500s – there were new thoughts and ideas too. There was a name for this time – a new name – the Reformation, and it was only just beginning.

Now, although there weren't newspapers at that time, in 1513 news was still important and in many ways it was the same sort of news that we see in print today.

Famous people died, new laws were passed, people fought to retain their independence while others fought to take that independence away. Large nations like France sought to make alliance with small countries like Scotland and it was this particular alliance that led to one of 1513's international incidents – a bloodthirsty battle. The news that was sent by foot messengers one September morning was a triumph for some, but disaster for others. When England attacked France, France's ally, Scotland, attacked England. The battle that day meant a brilliant victory for England, but a slaughtered army and a dead king for Scotland. The news was cheered south of the border, but many Scottish towns and villages wept over the outcome ... Haddington included.

Haddington was small, but strategically placed in the lowlands of Scotland. It was in the middle of a piece of land that was disputed territory between Scotland and England. During its history it had been attacked and razed to the ground more than once. In the year 1513, Haddington again suffered the consequences of being on the losing side of a battle. Many families lost sons, wives became widows, and children never saw their fathers again.

Earlier in 1513, one Haddington family received good news – a son had been born to carry on their name. Then, that September they received bad news as the father of that son was killed by the English troops.

The family was called Knox and the young boy's name was John.

Nobody saw fit to write down the date of his birth. Perhaps John's birthday became a day that the Knox family chose to forget. There may have been too many heartbreaking memories attached to a time that changed their lives so drastically.

However, the baby whose birthday was forgotten grew up to become one of the most important people of his era. Hundreds of years after his death the ordinary people of Scotland would look back on John Knox as a man to whom they personally owed a great debt ... and not only the people of Scotland. His influence spread across the whole of the Western World.

John Knox came into a world where education was a privilege for the rich and well off; where the Roman Catholic Church owned half of Scotland's wealth and where democracy was pretty much unheard of. In fact, the Roman Catholic Church at that time was eighteen times more wealthy than the Scottish monarchy. However, it is because of Knox's influence that Scotland brought free education to all its children. Two hundred years after Knox's death, the American declaration of independence was signed – a document greatly influenced by Knox's heart and pen. One passionate Scottish preacher has so influenced the world we inhabit today, that we can thank him and his God for many of our liberties in education, government and religion.

This man who is portrayed today, 500 years after his birth, as dour, bitter and hypocritical couldn't be further from that deceptive description. He was strong, fearless, passionate and full of surprises. Let's find out about the first surprise – John Knox the bodyguard.

Sword Practice

The early morning sun glinted off the great two-handed sword that was being brandished within the courtyard of Hugh Douglas of Longniddry. It wasn't being done in the name of violence, merely practice, as the young man with deep grey eyes and a serious expression tried to reacquaint himself with his country's chosen method of defence. Two young lads watched eagerly as their tutor, John Knox, thrust the blade with some skill into imaginary assailants.

'If you're thinking that this is going to make me forget your lessons, young sirs, then you are wrong.' John adjusted his stance before sweeping the large sword up and then down in a long arc. Deftly changing it from one hand to the other he altered his direction, thrusting the weapon briefly before standing back and doing it once again.

It wasn't exactly cold that morning, but John's breath still rose in clouds as his body warmed and the exercise made his heart pump. The sharp smell of horses and the sweet smell of hay pricked his nostrils. Gradually, a small drip of sweat broke out on his forehead. His body was beginning to work – something he had not been that used to lately. Tutoring the two young lads, avidly watching him from the sidelines, had been his main focus.

The impressive Douglas dwelling towered above them. It had been made to look more like a fortification than a family home, for that had been and still was, its main purpose. It could throw a gloomy shadow and was certainly large and foreboding. Some referred to it as Longniddry Castle. Although there were no royalty living there, the family was noble and respected by the ordinary folk.

A shiver edged its way down John's spine as he lifted the sword for another swipe. He stopped. Something made him take a long careful look across the countryside. 'It's best to be on my guard. I'll need to make that a habit now.' Even the Douglas family these days were becoming more cautious. Life was dangerous. John Knox knew that it made sense to keep your eyes open and your wits about you.

Seeing that there wasn't even a stray dog on the horizon, Knox got back to his training. He took a long look at his weapon, casting his gaze down the edge. It was a fine piece of craftsmanship and in the right pair of hands, could be lethal. However, it wouldn't be the Douglas family Knox would be protecting in the next few weeks; it would be the preacher, George Wishart, the name on everyone's tongue. Some looked on him as a dangerous reformer, others respected him as a powerful preacher.

The two young Douglas boys had barely moved an inch, they were so focussed on the sword that Knox held. Francis and his younger brother would soon be called upon to wield weapons like this themselves. Knox feared for their safety. What kind of world would they grow up in? Would they live to see a Scotland at liberty to think, speak and worship? They had been born into a family that followed the Reformed faith, that obeyed the Word of God before the demands of priests. John knew that families like that were not looked on with favour by the crown or the church. In the current climate, it could mean a death sentence. John shook his head in disbelief. Others had died for their faith before now, and Scotland was getting worse rather than better. Thrusting his sword with a touch more savagery than before, John turned one way then the next.

Stopping to catch his breath, he wiped away the sweat from his brow. Perhaps it was time to return the blade to its scabbard, but he could see how disappointed the young lads were. Francis and his younger brother did not want to go back to the classroom just yet. 'They probably hope to have a shot of the sword themselves,' John smiled. 'But they are too young to hold a weapon of this weight and power,' he reminded himself. 'I'm the one who needs the practice so let's give them something to look at ....' But before he could swing the sword back into action, young Francis piped up with, 'Is that really George Wishart's sword?'

'It is indeed. I believe it will do the job,' John surmised.

'What job is that exactly?' Francis asked.

John grinned – he knew these boys well by now – this was another delaying tactic. 'So, my lads, do you want a story of adventure instead of studies?'

Francis nodded eagerly. John rubbed a bit of dirt off one of his boots before starting his tale, 'Well, you know who Mr Wishart, is don't you?'

'He's in the study with Father as we speak, I believe, and he has visited a couple of times, perhaps more,' Francis replied.

'Well,' John continued, 'Wishart is a preacher of God's Word, blessed with courage and God's Holy Spirit. His calling is to spread God's Word around this country of ours – but many would stop him if they could and some have tried. I've been given this sword on Mr Wishart's request and with your father's permission. Mr Wishart is in need of some protection as he makes his way about this land. He has enemies who would take him prisoner, if not attack him, and kill him. It's my responsibility to accompany him, to draw my sword should anyone attempt to take the man's life.'

'Why, what is it that he has done?' the younger brother enquired.

Francis laughed in derision, but Knox just smiled.

'It is not what he has done, for he has done nothing wrong, nothing to justify the threats of these evil minded men.' Knox lowered himself onto a milk stool that had been left out by one of the maids. 'It is what he thinks and says and believes that has made him enemies.'

'Can thoughts put you in prison?' Francis asked, puzzled and slightly worried.

'They can in this year of our Lord 1545. I myself have had to leave behind the priesthood to be a tutor to you boys simply because I can no longer serve the Church of Rome. I believe it to be a false church. It is not the church of Christ, but a church of idols.' Taking out a rag, John began to wipe down the sword while warming to his subject. 'It is through hearing George Wishart preach and discussing these issues with him, that I have been brought to understand the truth.' Raising up the sword again to see the glow of the morning sun glint against its burnished side, John nodded his head solemnly. 'And it may be that I will have to raise this blade in the defence of truth, in the defence of one who speaks it with clarity and courage. Boys, I see it as a great honour to go ahead of George Wishart as his defender. By God's grace, I will be one of the Almighty's tools to bring truth to this land of ours.'

'Are you afraid?' the younger Douglas boy asked.

'There are times, young sir, when I am afraid,' John admitted. 'But I trust in God. He is our Sovereign Lord and there is nothing that is outside of his control. Wishart has taught me that – and more.'

Looking both of his charges in the face, he smiled. They hung on his every word in much the same way as he listened to Wishart. But he was forgetting himself, 'Francis, show your brother a good example by returning to the classroom and getting on with that Latin preparation I gave you. It's not long before I will have to leave with Mr Wishart to his next preaching venue. I will be back before the month is out. There are other lessons and readings that you are to continue with while I'm away and on your father's instruction

I am to test you both thoroughly on my return. Work hard while I'm gone and do not forget to pray for the safety of Mr Wishart as he and I travel to do God's work.'

Francis and his brother resigned themselves to the duty of study once again, but as they returned to the classroom, Francis looked back to see his tutor making ready for departure. He had such a desire to go with him, to experience adventure, to listen to more of John's stories, perhaps to witness Mr Knox beat the stuffing out of a couple of bandits. Now that would be fine! But the classroom was all that awaited him that day. 'Maybe on Mr Knox's return he will let me hold the sword for some practice.' He could but hope.

Wishart and Knox

Once John Knox had returned his sword to its scabbard and picked up his satchel of provisions, he set off to meet with Hugh Douglas of Longniddry, the boys' father. The Laird wished to say his farewells to both Knox and Wishart, before they set off on their journey.

He knocked politely on the door to his master's study, waited to hear the customary word 'enter' and then walked in. Hugh Douglas was standing smoking a pipe by the fireside and George Wishart was eagerly explaining to his patron the purpose of his journey.

'It's barely been a year since I returned to Scotland, but already I see that I should have been about this business earlier. Don't misunderstand me, Lord Douglas, my time in Switzerland was of great benefit and I am certain I would not be the man I am today, if it were not for the fact that I studied the Reformed faith there. But I've returned to this country to find it in such dire need spiritually.'

Hugh Douglas nodded solemnly, 'You are right, Wishart, without a doubt. I myself am of the Reformed faith and seek to bring my sons up in those ways which is why we have employed Mr Knox here to tutor them. However, I am concerned about this country of ours and the struggles my sons will have to face as they live as God's men in this land. There is much need for those like you to preach the truth with courage. It's Mauchline you're going to this time? You've been there before of course.'

George nodded, 'Yes, we'll be visiting some other places too, so there will be a lot of travel involved. However, I am looking forward to it. With Knox as my swordsman and companion we will have much godly conversation and meditation on the Word of God. Also, I will be better placed to think on the things of God, if I don't have to worry about the bandits that might jump out from round the next corner.'

'Or the priest or the cardinal,' Lord Douglas added.

George laughed quietly. 'I don't see the cardinal making the time to despatch me from this earth – but he could send a priest to do his dirty work. You are right, Lord Douglas – it is more likely to be a man of the cloth than a vagabond of the road who will attempt to send me to an early grave. That is another reason that I am glad to have Mr Knox. I've seen him practice with that blade. It may be in its scabbard now, but it is a fierce weapon in his hands. With God's protection, and this man's skill, I am as safe as I can ever be. And now that he has arrived with his sword and satchel to hand, we should be on our way.'

With that George and John bowed to Lord Douglas before retreating from the room and heading to the open road. George smiled at his bodyguard and exclaimed, 'It is a beautiful morning to be about the Lord's work, is it not?'

John nodded in agreement. 'I'm sure my two charges would agree. The lads looked reluctant to be going back to their studies this morning. A long walk in the country would suit them better. They see my sword and long for adventure – they have no inkling that with adventure comes danger.'

George Wishart nodded as they turned the corner from the house onto the road. 'Yes, young lads often do not see the need of study. I myself have always enjoyed it – I'm more of a thoughtful man than one who actively seeks thrills or risks. You, of course, have some knowledge of the danger of swords, as well as the excitement that is attached to them.'

John looked at George after he said this. He had heard George's preaching several times now, in chapels and abbeys around the country. There was something about Wishart that took his breath away, something he had not seen in any other preacher. There were times when George seemed to know exactly the right words to say. It was uncanny how he would say something, almost prophetic. Even this little question he had asked of John seemed to show how George Wishart just knew things and people. It was a gift.

Yes, John certainly knew about the danger of swords. 'You're right, George. I come from Haddington,' John replied.

'Ah, yes … Haddington is a place familiar with the sword.' George knew, as most people in Scotland did at that time, that Haddington was one of those places in the disputed lands between Scotland and England. It had seen its fair share of fighting.

'My family had personal experience of the grief of battle,' John continued. 'My father's name is on the list of the dead from Flodden. As a lad I was used to the sound of soldiers' tramping boots going one way or the other across our town.'

'Was it as a young lad you learned to wield the sword then?' George quizzed.

'Yes, swordsmanship is one skill that most young men, in a war-weary town, are taught. But my family had plans for me that didn't involve the battlefield. I was always meant for the church and an education.'

'That means you've come from a family with some means. If you send a lad to university it means that you're not poor.'

'We were, by God's grace, well off,' John admitted. 'Though we're not from a noble family I've had a good education. Have I told you that I went to St Andrews to study?'

George nodded as John carried on with his story. 'Well, I came out from that city with the skills that are necessary to work as a lawyer and notary. I became a priest some time later and it's only recently that I've given up that profession – largely under the influence of yourself, Mr Wishart, and your preaching. I believe that the Lord Jesus Christ is the only Saviour, and that he is mine. When I look at the Church of Rome and what they worship instead of our Lord, it sickens me. Statues of saints, relics, vials of the virgin Mary's milk, fingers of this or that disciple.'

'What you say gladdens my heart, John,' George interrupted. 'My time in Switzerland has acquainted me with many who follow the Reformed faith, including John Calvin. In fact, what you said reminds me of something Calvin wrote … how there are so many pieces of the cross in abbeys across Europe that whole forests would not contain the trees required to produce them. There are fingers and skulls and other pieces of the disciples worshipped as relics, that mean that the Apostle Peter must have been blessed with several heads and multiple hands.'

John laughed. The conversation was warming up and it indeed looked as though it would be an interesting and entertaining journey.

'I'm looking forward to visiting Mauchline again, are you?' Knox asked.

'Ah, John, it thrills my heart to be returning there. Do you remember how our first day at the place started off with very little promise? We had arrived at the Kirk and were barred from entry. I thought that was that at first. Some of the men with us would have beaten down the door to gain access to the building, but thankfully I managed to persuade them otherwise.'

'How exactly did you do that again? If I remember there was one man, Hugh Campbell of Kinyeancleuch, who was being particularly bothersome?'

'Yes, John, that's right. His heart was in the right place, but I remember I took him aside quietly and told him, "Brother, Christ Jesus is as potent upon the fields as in the Kirk. He himself oftener preached in the desert and at the seaside, than he did in the temple of Jerusalem."'

'That is so true,' John exclaimed eagerly. 'And then that was what you did – you followed in the footsteps of Christ in more ways than one. You preached God's Word and in the open air.'

'Yes, and didn't God bless us! The congregation withdrew to a small stone wall, at the south-west side of Mauchline, upon which I climbed up, with some help from you I remember. Everyone was either sitting or standing round about me. It was by the grace of God that it wasn't cold and wet that day.'

John smiled. 'Yes. I remember how the sun was shining and the wind was light and balmy; a perfect day for preaching in the open air.'

George ran his fingers through his hair. 'I felt the presence of God with me that day as I preached …,' he sighed. 'And then at the end of the sermon I saw a man, Laurence Rankin the local laird, standing in front of me, tears flooding his face, sobs catching in his throat. Many of the men and women there that day stared at him in astonishment.'

'I was one of them,' John exclaimed. 'You don't often see a grown man cry like that, far less the local laird. He was well known in the area as a truly wicked man. Yet that day the Lord God touched his heart and converted him from a life of sin to a sure and free salvation. Have you heard anything from him since?'

'I have not heard from the laird personally, but from others. I recall that on that day there were people who looked at his tears and muttered, "We'll see." And it is true that some conversions turn out to be hypocrisy, but not in this case. I've not long received a letter from one of the believers there and it provides all the proof I need. The man's life and conversation are witness to the fact that he was truly converted. Thanks be to God.'

'Amen,' John replied.

That day had been one of those remarkable moments in the life of George Wishart. One that John would remember for the rest of his life. A day where one man, one soul, was brought to Christ. John prayed eagerly as they went along, that they would see more people rescued from sin during their travels.

George kept up with John's steady pace, but John could see that the preacher's thoughts were elsewhere. 'Let him think,' John admonished himself. 'Don't disturb him if you don't have to. It could well be these thoughts that bring God's Word to lost souls tonight at our lodgings. I'll keep an eye on the horizon, while he keeps his thoughts in the Word.'

An hour or so after they'd stopped for a bite to eat from their satchels and a fresh drink of water from a stream, John decided that he'd better interrupt George's thoughts – just briefly. 'There's still quite a way to go, George, I'm afraid we're going to have to increase our pace if we hope to arrive before nightfall.' George nodded and increased his pace while singing a psalm gently to himself. A verse or two later, John joined in. Fresh air, godly conversation and now music – he did indeed have great reason to praise God.

A Plague and a Priest

Some weeks later, John had returned to Longniddry
and was trying to enthuse Francis and his brother with
their education. There had been several journeys with
George to various parishes across the country. Nothing
eventful had happened. Not even a fox or a wild cat
had barred their way. John was beginning to realise,
however, that the real predators were the priests and
cardinals. He suspected that these men were hunting
for prey – and amongst that prey was Wishart.

Since their last expedition, George had gone
to preach in Kyle and then when the plague had hit
Dundee, he had immediately made his way there to
give what comfort he could to the afflicted population.

Later, in Hugh Douglas's study, John exclaimed,
'It's just like Wishart. I know he says that he doesn't
seek danger, but he is taking a great risk all the same.
He is putting his life on the line in order to save
others.'

Lord Douglas turned to face Knox, 'But, John, it's
not just their bodies, but their souls. That's why it's so
important.'

John nodded. That was Wishart's real motivation –
to bring lost souls to Christ. 'I hear that the plague is
so powerful in Dundee, it almost passes belief,' Knox
added. 'The number of people dying increases every

twenty-four hours. I worry for Wishart being in such a place of pestilence.'

Douglas reached over to his desk and brought out a couple of letters, 'Listen to this, John. George wrote me just before he left for Dundee. "They are now in trouble and need comfort. Perhaps the hand of God will make them magnify and reverence that Word which before, for fear of men, they set at light price." He is there to be God's instrument, to save lost souls and to bring what comfort he can to these poor people.'

'Then,' Lord Douglas deftly filled another pipe before laying another letter out in front of Knox, 'I received this today. He gives an account of his preaching to the plague victims in Dundee. He stood at the head of the East Port of the town – the sick on one side and the whole on the other. Here, John, you can take a look, there's nothing confidential in it.'

John eagerly took the letter from Douglas's hand, to read how his friend had preached on a verse from Psalm 107. 'He sent his Word and healed them.' In the sermon, George spoke of the benefits of God's Word and the danger to those who treated it with contempt. Many that day realised that death was not something to be feared for the believer, but rather a blessing for those who departed trusting in God's salvation.

That night, as John returned to his room, he marvelled at the account of how George was not only preaching, but seeing to the physical needs of the sick and dying too. 'Many would be too afraid to touch someone with the plague. They would fear for their own life,' John thought as he wrapped himself in his covers. The letter had said, 'The poor are now no more neglected than were the rich.' That was something indeed, and so typical of George Wishart. It only amazed John more, that George still had enemies. 'May our Lord protect him,' John whispered as he lay his head down for sleep.

'Come on now, lads, settle down. Your attitude is not conducive to study. I'll have no more of this rowdy behaviour in the classroom,' John admonished the two Douglas boys as he entered the schoolroom to the noise of abundant chatter. 'You're louder than the fishwives on market day.'

Francis then turned to John and gasped, 'You haven't heard!'

'Heard what?' John asked, confused about what piece of news could have caused such a hullaballoo.

'Someone tried to assassinate Mr Wishart! Father got a letter.'

Just then a servant entered the classroom with an instruction for John to make his way to the study.

John told the boys to translate a particular piece of Greek text and then he hurried down to find out what had happened. Lord Douglas was at his writing desk, quill in hand.

'Come in, John, come in. You'll have heard from the boys no doubt the news I received this morning.'

'The boys mentioned the attempt on Wishart's life, sir, when your servant came with the message. I don't think I have heard the full account.'

'Very well – I'll fill you in on what's happened. It sends chills down my spine when I think of that conversation we had some months ago. Do you remember when George referred to the fact that the cardinal wouldn't dirty his hands by attacking him, but that he might send a priest to do his dirty work? It appears that's exactly what has happened.'

'How can that be, Lord Douglas?' John urged.

'George had just finished preaching and as the congregation made to leave, a priest was seen to be standing on the steps. Nobody suspected anything, but he had a concealed weapon. Then, and this is the amazing thing, George seemed to know what the man was about to do. He went right up to him and grabbed him by the arm. 'My friend,' he said, 'what are you doing?' Immediately, he took the weapon off him and the priest, so ashamed of himself, fell down at Wishart's feet and confessed the truth of the matter. All the sick, that surrounded the church, cried out to deliver the priest into their hands, so that they could take him by force. So what do you think Wishart did?'

John knew his friend and his tender heart. 'There's no way he would hand anyone, friend or enemy, over to a baying mob. I dare say that priest ended up under Wishart's protection.'

'Exactly!' Lord Douglas exclaimed. 'Wishart gathered the priest to him and declared to all that "whosoever troubles this man troubles me". He has not hurt me, but has done great comfort to us all. We now understand what it is that we fear. In the future we will watch better.'

'And he'll need to — that's all I can say,' Lord Douglas declared. 'That priest has proved one thing — we were right to be so afraid for George. I'd be far happier if he was under my protection again, rather than ministering to plague victims and showing sympathy to would-be murderers.'

'You said yourself,' John pointed out, 'it is their souls he is burdened for. And anyway, he may yet return to these parts,' John suggested.

Lord Douglas nodded slowly, 'That is true, John. You do well to remind me of these lost souls. And I have heard that Wishart plans to make a short break at the end of the year to your old town. He plans to preach a series of sermons there and it is possible that for some of that time, he could be persuaded to stay under my roof.'

'Haddington?' John exclaimed. He wondered for a moment if he might meet George there. These days, as well as being tutor at Longniddry, he had taken on some duties as Scripture reader at Haddington.

It appeared that Lord Douglas had the same idea.

'If you can leave the boys some studies to be getting on with, it might be good if you were to visit George at Haddington this winter. The church will probably need you as Scripture reader there over the next few weeks.' A frown passed over Lord Douglas's brow. 'Reacquaint yourself with that old two-handed sword. I doubt George really knows how to use it himself. What do you think?'

'I would like nothing better, but to see our friend George once more.'

'Very good,' Lord Douglas took a long puff on his pipe. 'I understand that his first night at Haddington will be spent within the town, but that his second night will be spent at Lethington with Sir Richard Maitland. He's a supporter of the Reformation, but I am not certain that he is a believer. He'll make you both welcome, however. Perhaps the Cockburns will also play host to him for some time at Ormiston House.'

John nodded with agreement, 'The Cockburns are a fine family. John Cockburn has been a friend to me these past years; as good a friend to me as you yourself have been.'

Lord Douglas looked pleased at the compliment. 'Yes, Cockburn is a good man and converted. I dare say all these men will gladly look after George when he stays in the area – and you, of course. It will be good for George to have his old bodyguard to hand. When he arrives make sure he understands that there is a warm welcome for him here at Longniddry.'

John nodded – excited and eager about the journey that was to come and finally meeting his good friend and mentor once again.

The Winter's End

When the snow began to thicken and the winter festivities were in full swing, John left his pupils with some studies to be getting on with. They, however, took to throwing snowballs and running about with sledges the moment their tutor had packed his bags. John smiled as he exited the gates of the Douglas home to the sound of a full blown snowball fight. He relished the prospect of meeting Wishart again – and after a fairly quick journey, he wasn't disappointed.

'John, my friend,' George exclaimed, 'how good to see you. It has been too long, but we will enjoy catching up.'

'Yes, indeed, and I will enjoy hearing you preach once more.'

'Yes, I am to preach here in Haddington for a while … I have several sermons prepared already. It would be good if I could discuss them with you.' Over the next couple of weeks, Knox and Wishart discussed life, faith, politics, and the Word of God, but over time something in Wishart's tone of voice made John puzzled. There seemed to be something more solemn than usual in his speech.

'What's the matter, George?' John quizzed.

George just smiled a gentle smile and told his friend not to be concerned. But by and by, John found out what the problem was. The rumours were true – George's enemies were on the prowl. 'I've had a fairly reliable report that the Earl of Bothwell is against me. He has many men in his command and is well connected to the Queen Mother. He could be a real danger. There are others who say he is just a puppy of royalty with no backbone … but I'm not sure. It may be that I will have support from friends in the West. I am hoping for some correspondence soon which will promise me help should I need it.'

'I hope that correspondence will come soon,' John exclaimed, 'if only to put your mind at rest.'

'Thank you, John, but I need to take my own preaching to heart and "Trust in the Lord". He is the best way to put any troubled mind at rest and to soothe any worried soul.'

Then, one evening, just before Wishart was about to preach, John was summoned to his side. George held a piece of paper in his hand. 'It is not good news, John. I got this letter the other day and have been praying over it for some time now. The Lords of Kyle in the West will not come to my support. I have been abandoned. I am wearied of this world for I perceive that the men in it now begin to be weary of God.'

It was unusual for Wishart to enter into conversation just before preaching. It was usually a time that George withdrew into his thoughts and prayers. Knox didn't really understand what his friend was saying.

He turned to George and said, 'I'll leave you for the present so that you can think upon your sermon.'

But John kept an eye on him in the meantime. For half an hour George paced up and down behind the High Altar.

'I hope when it comes to the time to preach he has a good congregation to listen to him,' John thought. Since Wishart's arrival in Haddington the numbers attending the church services had steadily dwindled. It was nothing to do with Wishart's preaching – John knew that. There was something more sinister afoot.

When Wishart climbed the steps to the pulpit, the congregation was considerably smaller than any of the previous weeks – and those weeks hadn't been that great. The local population had been discouraged from coming to hear Wishart by the Earl of Bothwell. He was the overlord of the whole region and people genuinely feared him. He owned a lot of the land and property in the area and had the power to force people off crofts and out of businesses.

During that evening service, George Wishart preached to the few who had dared to come to hear him. 'Sore and fearful shall the plagues be that shall come upon this place because of its contempt,' George Wishart announced.

John shivered as he heard George continue to proclaim that in the years to come, strangers would possess this town and that its locals would be chased from their dwelling places. 'This will take place because they have not had the courage to come to the house of God to hear God's Word preached.' George's gaze circled the whole congregation, as if he could look into the soul of each person present.

John wondered if this is what he was doing. He knew that there had been times when George Wishart's word had come to pass. Perhaps this would be one of them.

Finally, the wearied and discouraged preacher left the pulpit to make his way to Ormiston House and the hospitality of the Cockburns. Several of the local gentry, who followed the Reformed faith, would also be guests there that night. John looked forward to some spiritual conversation with George and these other believers, but after the evening meal George decided that he needed an early night.

'He's going to bed earlier than usual,' Lord Douglas said to the group as Wishart's footsteps retreated along the corridor. 'Today must have really challenged him. A night's rest is what he needs. I pray to God that he gets it. Perhaps I'll follow his example,' Lord Douglas yawned and rubbed his eyes. 'Goodnight friends, sleep well.'

However, nobody got a sound night's sleep that night. Before the moon reached its height the violent rhythm of hoofbeats could be heard on the snow covered soil outside. Armour glinted in the moonlight and the steaming breath of hard-ridden horses rose up in clouds. The Earl of Bothwell and his troops quickly surrounded John Cockburn's house. Bothwell announced to Cockburn that the Governor and the Cardinal were on their way, but that if Cockburn surrendered George Wishart into his hands then he would personally see to it that the Cardinal did not harm Wishart in any way. Bothwell even promised this on his honour and in the presence of God – so George was delivered into his hands.

Just at that moment, John Knox seemed to realise the danger of the situation. Grasping the sword that had been Wishart's protection for so many journeys, he made to take it out of its scabbard. For so long he had practiced for this very occasion – but just as the blade was struck by the moonlight, George turned to his friend and said, 'One life is enough for a sacrifice, Mr Knox. Go back to those lads and God bless you.'

Wishart reached out and gently withdrew the sword from Knox's grasp. Knox did not stop him. The reality struck home that there was nothing he could do. Laying into the Earl of Bothwell and his troops would be certain death for Knox and Wishart.

'Where are they taking him?' John demanded.

'I've heard one of the soldiers mention Edinburgh,' a servant whispered into John's ear. 'That will mean that he'll most likely be imprisoned in Edinburgh Castle.'

Just then the Earl swung his horse around in a circle and with a call to his troops, commanded the company to make haste.

Wishart turned to wave farewell to his friends … but it was just for a moment … for shortly after he had disappeared into the black night. A nagging doubt ate into Knox's soul – the expression on his friend's face made him think that Wishart knew he would not be back.

As the sound of Earl Bothwell's horses diminished into the darkness, those who had been eating their meal with George Wishart only a few hours previously stood aghast. They looked at the spot in the pitch black where they had last caught sight of their friend. Had it really happened? Was there anything they could have done differently? The very idea that Wishart had been carted off by an ally of Cardinal Beaton was hard to believe. What did men of power and might want with him?

As the guests at Ormiston House made their way back inside, questions and exclamations echoed around the walls. It wasn't just Wishart who was being taken away by the Earl's troops. Some of Bothwell's men remained to escort Cockburn and the other noblemen to the castle prison too. Knox looked around anxiously for Lord Douglas but he was nowhere to be seen.

While servants and grooms were being despatched to collect some basic possessions for the prisoners to take with them, Cockburn had suggested that the remainder of Bothwell's troops should feed their horses and take some refreshment themselves. They didn't require much persuading when glasses of port were handed round, and some delicious cold meats and pastries were laid out on the dining room table.

John couldn't bare to see the soldiers eating and making merry, so he gruffly retreated to his quarters. Why weren't Cockburn and others plotting an ambush? Didn't any of them care for George Wishart's safety? But John realised that would be foolhardy. There was no way they could carry off an attack of that magnitude.

There were some really powerful people behind these arrests. John was certain of it. It had the stink of the Queen Mother – Mary de Guise behind it. 'That she-wolf has her claws everywhere these days,' John grimaced. Everyone knew that Bothwell would do anything for her, it was quite a scandal at the palace – a man who had abandoned his wife was now playing court to the widow of the King of Scotland. If anything convinced John of the need for God's Word in his own country it was the immorality of the throne, or those close to it. At least Mary de Guise wasn't reigning – but a little girl not even five years old couldn't hold the sceptre and wear the crown with any presence or authority. Her mother was queen in all but name.

John sighed. Would this land ever be somewhere that God's Word was respected and obeyed – where justice and godliness reigned rather than greed and immorality? Knox stood at the frosted window pane of his bedroom, staring out into the night. This country of his was under lock and key to grasping gentry and callous cardinals. The very idea that that French woman, Mary de Guise, was the power behind the throne chilled him to the bone. There had been talk at one point of marrying the young princess to Prince Edward – Henry VIII's son. But nothing had come of it. Mary de Guise had done all she could to ensure that her young daughter did not go south of the border. 'She's got other plans for that little girl and if I'm not mistaken they involve an ocean journey to another throne,' John muttered under his breath.

The sound of yells and shouts came from the courtyard below. John opened the window and looked quickly out – the shape of a man could be seen running towards the trees. Two of Bothwell's men were in hot pursuit.

'It's Lord Brunstane,' came a whisper just behind him. John jumped in fright. He had not known anyone was in the room with him. Cockburn stood behind him in a riding cloak.

'Calm yourself, John,' John Cockburn patted him on the shoulder. 'It's just me. We decided that Brunstane had the best chance of making a break for it. He's fleet of foot and strong. He's fitter than the rest of us and will soon shake Bothwell's men on a night like this. With most of the soldiers now departed we saw that there was a slim opportunity for one of our number to make a run for it.'

'What about Lord Douglas?' John asked anxiously.

'We've hidden him. He's safe for now. At first light he's going to walk across the fields and hide in that copse by the chapel. Then you're to leave with my son, Alexander – taking care not to be seen if at all possible. You'll pick Lord Douglas up and make your way back to Longniddry. I've asked Hugh if he'll take responsibility for my son while I'm in prison. I'm afraid that things are going to get a lot worse for the Reformed faith before they ever get any better. I can make arrangements for my wife and the other children to stay for now with her parents. If Alexander goes with you to Longniddry then he'll be under Douglas's protection and you'll be able to keep him at his studies. Alexander is my heir,' Cockburn said, anxiety sounding in his urgent whispers. 'He needs to be protected and to continue to be moulded into the man God wants him to be. I've seen the way you are with Hugh's boys – I want you to be that influence on my son too.'

John nodded slowly. It would be an honour to tutor another young lad in the ways of the Saviour.

As Lord Cockburn made to go to the door John asked, 'And Wishart?'

'Don't get your hopes up, John,' he replied. 'He will be taken to Edinburgh Castle, but I believe they'll move him quickly to St Andrews.'

'To Cardinal Beaton?' John asked, though he knew the answer.

'Yes, that's what I've heard. It may be some will try a rescue – but I doubt it. It would be certain death for any who attempted it. I'm afraid it will be the bottle-dungeon for George.'

John sighed. He had heard of the bottle-dungeon – everyone had. It was the infamous St Andrews prison that was shaped like a bottle. A narrow neck at the top and then steep sloping sides that plunged twenty-five feet to the bottom. Hard, rugged rock all the way.

The following morning, while it was still dark, John and Alexander Cockburn, the eldest son of the Lord of Ormiston, quietly slipped away. Stealthily, they made their way towards the old chapel where Lord Douglas, a bit dishevelled looking, crept out from the copse and mounted the horse behind Alexander. They made their way by back roads avoiding the prying eyes of villagers until, at last, they arrived, safe and well at Longniddry.

Francis and his younger brother were both delighted to see Alexander and as the three boys got reacquainted, Lord Douglas ushered John into his study. Hugh Douglas was ashen faced as he shook his head in disbelief. 'I can't believe it has happened. Lord Cockburn and I have suspected Bothwell for some time now, but we never thought he would do anything. We knew his sympathies were with Mary de Guise, but he's such a weak man I never thought he would have the audacity to do what he did. Can you credit it – he's not only arrested George Wishart but Lord Cockburn himself.'

John interrupted. 'There's Lord Calder too, and Brunstane who made his escape through the woods.'

Douglas sighed. 'Let's hope Brunstane lies low for a bit. I really can't see there is anything that I can do for the others. I'm afraid Wishart will be outwith my influence completely. He will certainly be in St Andrews before the end of the month.'

And in fact the news that came from one of Hugh Douglas's messengers some time later was that George Wishart was indeed in the dungeon at St Andrews; Lord Burnstane was still in hiding, but Lord Calder and Cockburn were free.

Hugh Douglas frowned as he read the message aloud to John in the study, 'Calder compromised – he's agreed to support the cardinal. That's not an honourable outcome for him, I'm afraid. But listen to this … Cockburn freed himself by leaping the walls of the castle right in the middle of the day. He's on the run but he's free.'

John laughed with relief, 'If I may, sir, let me return to the classroom to pass on the good news to young Alexander. He'll be overjoyed.'

Lord Douglas gave Knox his permission and suggested that it might be a good idea to let the boys run off some energy. 'With all this excitement you won't get that much study out of the boys today.'

John admitted this was probably quite a good idea.

Through the cold months of January and February, Wishart remained in the dungeon waiting for his trial. Then in March he was brought before Cardinal Beaton and the Archbishop of Glasgow. These two men hated each other's guts, but were willing to put it all behind them in order to put George Wishart to death. The day after his trial, Wishart was sentenced to be strangled and burnt. It was March 1st.

When the news of George Wishart's sentence reached his friends in Longniddry, John hung his head. Lord Douglas read the letter out with some difficulty. 'His final words were to the crowd who had come to watch, many to give some last bit of courage and strength. "Do not be horrified by my death, but watch my face for you will not see it change." It did not.'

John taught his pupils as normal that day, although he sensed they didn't feel like it. It wasn't that the boys wanted to be running around after a ball, or building a den in the woods, they didn't have the stomach for that either. It was as though the news they had received that morning had destroyed every last spark of hope or joy or strength within them.

John then remembered the words George had preached at the East Port of Dundee – the fit and well on one side and the sick and dying on the other. 'It is neither herb nor plaster, O Lord, but thy Word that healeth all.'

'Yea Lord – and broken hearts too?' John pondered.

After this thought John did for his lads what he would do for many people in the months and years to come – turn them to the Word of God and to the comfort of a sure and free salvation in Christ their Lord.

And then he opened his Bible where he often opened it at times of particular difficulty and trouble: John 17.

As he read verse twenty-four aloud to the three sorrowful students he himself caught a glimpse of what joys his friend George Wishart was now experiencing. This prayer of his Saviour's for those who believed in his name showed John Knox the joy of eternity that was reality for his friend and a certain hope for him some day ....

> *Father, I want those you have given me to be with me where I am, and to see my glory, the glory you have given me because you loved me before the creation of the world.*

A City Refuge

John could always tell when he had missed some exciting piece of news. He would enter the classroom to a cacophony of sound – young lads chattering loudly about what they had just heard or witnessed.

Early one morning John knew for sure that something was afoot. He opened the door to see Alexander throwing the younger Douglas boy over a writing-desk, while Francis had taken a walking stick from his father's cupboard and was using it like a rapier, thrusting it at an imaginary villain who appeared, strangely enough, to be sitting in a chair.

'What is going on, boys?' John asked, trying to raise his voice above the racket.

'You haven't heard the news?' Francis asked, incredulously. 'Where have you been, Mr Knox?'

'Getting your lessons ready, while I was hoping you would be studying!'

Alexander raised his hand, tentatively, 'Mr Knox, I suppose you could say we were studying history as it was being made?'

'Really?' John seriously doubted this rather imaginative excuse. What he had just witnessed in the classroom seemed more like boisterous fun and games than actual study. However, his students soon showed him otherwise.

'Cardinal Beaton is dead,' the youngest Douglas boy gasped out as he extricated himself from underneath the desk.

Now that was news. The Cardinal had a vicious reputation amongst the Scottish Reformers. Many had been on the wrong side of his power – having been thrown into prison for simply expressing thoughts and opinions that were contrary to the Roman Catholic Church. When Knox heard the lads gasp out their exciting tale he privately acknowledged that perhaps Alexander had been right about history being made. Bit by bit, with some impromptu acting of the more gruesome scenes, the young lads told their tutor about the grizzly end of the St Andrews Cardinal.

For some months now, the Cardinal had been building and extending various parts of the castle at St Andrews. This required large amounts of limestone to be taken over the drawbridge. One morning, as further wagons were given access to the castle grounds, a small group of men just happened to wander in. Nobody stopped them. There were so many people coming and going due to the building works that nobody was suspicious when they saw some strange faces in the crowd.

However, when a second group and then a third crossed over the drawbridge, and one group asked if the Cardinal was awake, the porter got alarmed and tried to raise the drawbridge. That was when everything suddenly kicked off. One man knocked the porter on the head and then threw him into the moat – that was the bit that Alexander and the youngest

Douglas lad had been re-enacting when John entered the classroom.

As soon as the drawbridge was secure and other parts of the castle were under rebel control, some of the rebels began to make their way towards Cardinal Beaton's apartments. He was well awake by that time and knew that his life was in danger. With the help of a servant he began to try and barricade his door – but it was too little too late. The renegade forces knocked down the door and killed him as he sat in his chair yelling, 'I am a priest, ye dare not kill a priest.'

Over the following weeks it was suggested that John Knox went into hiding. The Douglas family also left Longniddry for a time. Hugh Douglas and his lads, as well as Alexander, headed for the hills in order to escape the reprisals from Mary de Guise's supporters. They hoped to meet up with Lord Cockburn once again as they sought shelter in caves and crofts in the surrounding hills. But as time passed, both Lord Douglas and Lord Cockburn began to see that a life on the run was not what they wanted for their boys.

They arranged a meeting with John at an abandoned farm house in the hills behind Longniddry. John made his way there through the mist. It was a long walk and even he felt tired when he caught sight of the house in the distance. 'I wonder how the boys are doing?' he thought to himself. He was eager to see his young students once more. The boys were pleased to see him too as they all rushed to the door when they heard his knock. John, however, was surprised at their appearance. The boys were thinner, looking and far dirtier than John had ever seen them. 'I probably don't look that clean myself,' John thought. 'I've also been on the run and haven't slept in my own bed for weeks. But these boys are in dire need of a wash and a normal home life ... not one of them will have opened a book since our last lesson. I'm certain of that!'

Straightaway, the boys' fathers shared with John their plan. They had also realised that their sons needed safety and stability. 'The city of St Andrews is no longer under the control of the Church of Rome. There has been a siege, but now it seems that the siege is broken. Mary de Guise's troops have dispersed and I have heard that some, of the Reformed faith, are making their way there to find refuge,' Hugh Douglas explained. 'Cockburn and I think it would be a good place for you to take our sons to. We don't propose to go to St Andrews ourselves. Our property is here and it is better that we remain in hiding while there is still a ransom on our heads.'

John thought for a moment, 'My Lords, are you certain that St Andrews is a refuge? Don't you think that the Queen Mother will, even as we speak, be mustering more troops in order to attack the town once again?'

'Perhaps, but we have it under good authority that if St Andrews was ever to be seriously attacked, Lord Somerset would come to support the rebels.'

John wasn't sure about that. 'Taking your sons into what could potentially be a dangerous situation, may not be a wise decision.' But John took another look at the three lads. The situation they were in at present would be the death of them before too long. 'Yet, you are right that your boys can't survive much longer on the moors. I myself do not want to be going this way and that across the country for much longer. Perhaps St Andrews is the best option. What about you? If I need to contact you for some reason what should I do?'

Lord Douglas sighed, 'That will be difficult. It will be more likely that we will contact you … but should the worst come to the worst Francis here knows how to get himself and the two lads to his aunt's home in the country. Even if they were to be captured and put in prison, their connections are good enough for them to avoid being thrown onto a galley ship … but God willing it will not come to that.'

John shivered at that thought. His connections were not so good. His young charges might be able to avoid that particular punishment – he wouldn't.

Cockburn looked John in the eye, 'I told you once before that I wanted you to be an influence for good on my son. It's not just how well you teach him Latin and Greek – it's how you teach him God's Word. I've nothing more to say … the boys are ready and packed. Are you willing to take them?'

'Aye, I'll take them,' John agreed. 'Best that you say your goodbyes now, lads, as we'll need to be on our way.'

Hugh Douglas gathered his sons to him for some last words of advice. Cockburn held Alexander fast, praying with him quietly before he pushed him away saying, 'God speed, my son. Trust in the Lord.'

And with that the two fathers disappeared at speed into the mist. John and the lads left just as quickly in the other direction.

'We've some long hard walking ahead of us,' John muttered as they made their way over the moor. 'You'll be glad of a Latin lesson at the end of this, I assure you.'

'Latin?' Francis muttered glumly. 'I'd almost forgotten what that was.'

Alexander laughed, 'Mr Knox will soon remind you, won't you, sir.'

'Aye, that I will,' John announced. 'There's nothing to stop me testing you on your grammar as we make our way.'

All three boys groaned inwardly …. 'I should have kept quiet,' Francis scolded himself.

As the tired and muddy students followed their tutor over the hills, they did a little study in grammar and mathematics. Knox didn't need quills or manuscripts to teach the boys – he had everything he needed to teach them in his head. Steadings and outhouses were their night-time accommodation. Their provisions were supplemented by whatever edible berries they could find. John occasionally set a trap for a rabbit, or lay still at the edge of a river as he guddled for a trout. All these skills he had learnt as a youngster. As they reached the brow of yet another hill and the spires and castle ramparts of St Andrews rose before them, the boys let out a great sigh of relief. That was when John decided to give his young charges a brief lesson about the town they would soon be staying in.

'What coast are we on, Francis?' John asked. This was a very basic question and one each of the lads should have been able to answer straightaway, but Francis ummed and scratched his head. 'Not good enough, lad. Even a youngster who has barely started his letters could answer that one.'

Francis grimaced and then, before his brother could beat him to it, he exclaimed, 'Of course – the East. I knew that. We're in Fife.'

'Well, you got there, eventually,' John muttered. 'Of course, you all know that this town is named after St Andrew, the apostle, and that the university was founded there sometime after 1410.'

Francis's brother remarked, 'I didn't know that.'

'Now you do, young man. Let's see if you can tell me this: Name two of the rivers connected to St Andrews.'

Alexander, who had been fairly quiet up till that point, responded, 'The Tay and the Eden.'

'Correct. This town, that we will call our home for however long God intends us to be here, has a great history. King Constantine built a church here in AD 877 and the burgh of St Andrews was represented at the Great Council in Scone Palace in 1357. It is recognised as the ecclesiastical capital of Scotland – and is at present under the control of the Reformed church.'

'Is it true that Cardinal Beaton's body still hangs over the ramparts?' Francis asked eagerly.

Knox sighed, 'No, I don't believe that to be true, Francis. It will have been taken down by now.'

'Aw,' the younger Douglas lad said in disappointment.

John just shook his head. 'They may come from noble families,' he thought to himself, 'but they're just like any lad you'll find on the farm or in the towns ... full of mischief and trouble if given a chance.'

Initially, as they'd made their way over the desolate mountains and moors, the little group had seen few travellers. Now, as they walked on the main roads to St Andrews, they regularly met with people fleeing in the same direction. Rumours of reprisals had been circulated and other Reformers and Protestants were making their way to the town. One man reeled off a list of people he had heard were already there, 'Sir Henry Balnaves; Sir James Balfour; Kirkcaldy, Laird of Grange ... there are many others too, but these are the better known gentry,' the old traveller exclaimed.

John nodded – well-known men all of them and Kirkcaldy was famous for his skill on the battlefield. Something that might come in useful if the other rumours he had heard turned out to be true.

He decided to ask the old traveller at his side if he had heard anything about the rumours of another siege or attack. 'Folks are talking about it,' the traveller replied, 'but I've seen no evidence for it as yet. On my travels I haven't seen any troop movements. I've kept my eyes peeled as we've walked along the coastal routes and there haven't been any top masts or sails on the horizon. No sign of friend or foe.'

'That's good then,' John replied. 'I'm concerned about my young charges and if we are going in the right direction for their safety,' Knox added this last bit quietly, just in case the lads were eavesdropping.

'The rebels that took the castle in the first place have decided that it's safer to stay than leave,' the old man informed Knox. 'I think that's a good indication that you are making the right decision. The lads here say that you're a man of the cloth yourself. Are you one of the Reformed faith then?'

'Yes, I am,' John agreed.

'Well, you'll be interested to hear that there is a godly preacher in St Andrews – that one they call "the heretic preacher" from Ayrshire, John Rough.'

'I look forward to meeting him,' John said, glad to hear that there was at least someone in charge of preaching the Word in that town.

Arriving in St Andrews, John soon realised that the old traveller's tale of there being no evidence of a siege or imminent attack wasn't quite right. The talk in the town was all of fight and intrigue.

The reformers were standing firm in the castle. The ramparts were being guarded. No one left or entered without permission. All visitors were checked and quizzed before they gained access. The tall imposing castle thrust itself up out of the dark cliff top and this was where John and his students were to stay. John asked to speak to the rebel, Henry Balnaves, on his arrival only to find out that he and one or two of the more prominent rebels had gone to seek help from the English King, Henry VIII.

'They must think then that there is a need for this. Are we to be attacked?' John asked the Ayrshire preacher, John Rough, who had come to introduce himself.

'Yes. They may come at us again. It is certain that Mary de Guise has sent to France for ships. Though there are no signs at the moment of troops – it's more than likely she's just biding her time. Henry VIII may be our last hope.'

'Do not speak in that way, sir. While we are still under God's care there is always hope. But I have heard that Henry VIII is not well and that he does not care much for the Scots. I do not think you will find him a supporter to your cause with coin or troops. If it was his young son, Edward, I might be more positive. I have heard good things about him. He has been brought up to study the Reformed faith. However, he is but a young lad and does not sit on the throne.'

'That is true but many are saying that it is his uncle, Lord Somerset, who will support us at St Andrews if the castle is attacked. Even if Edward was on the throne, it would be the power behind the throne we would have to look to.'

'Hmm,' John Knox grimaced. 'I don't know. I think it is wrong to put our trust in princes ... even godly ones. The Bible tells us that. We may spend the next months scanning the North Sea for signs of ships – not knowing if they be from the enemy or from a friend. But I'm glad we are here all the same. The boys were weary of moving from place to place and I'm relieved too to be able to settle down and tutor them.'

A few days later John bumped into the Ayrshire preacher once again.

'Are your lads settling into their lessons?' Rough asked.

'They're doing well, thank you. I've decided to teach them Calvin's catechism and they are going to recite these from memory in public in the parish church.'

'Oh! Delightful!' Rough exclaimed. 'I'm sure you'll get quite a few coming to listen. There's nothing the people like better than hearing children at their lessons.'

'That's true,' Knox replied. 'Over the years I've realised that teaching children is in fact a good way of teaching adults.'

'Well, Mr Knox, that is a smart idea – it is like killing two birds with one stone – which reminds me ... I've a stew of some fowl or other simmering over the hearth at my lodgings and you would be most welcome to come and join me.'

John eagerly agreed to the offer of a hot meal and followed Mr Rough to the quarters he was staying in. The castle was cramped, and everyone shared space and provisions – but Rough had found a small corner that was relatively peaceful and where the two men could sit down and enjoy food and fellowship together. After having enjoyed a delicious stew of something, which John thought might have been pigeon, he sat back to enjoy conversation with his new friend. Later on, John listened to some music as Mr Rough brought out his old wooden flute to play some favourite folk tunes.

John Knox relaxed in his chair, stretching out his legs as close to the fire as he could make them go. John

Rough then stole a quiet glance at the rugged face of his companion, the somewhat dour expression, the long expressive hands. People had already pre-judged the new refugee. John was criticised for being harsh and sullen … but Rough thought that people were too quick to make up their minds. He'd seen someone different tonight. John had sang the old ballads as well as anyone, joining in with the merry tunes and the sombre ones. Although Rough was an official preacher in the town, he could recognise the fact that John had a better gift with words than he had. 'If only I could get him to accept the vocation of preacher and pastor here. There is nobody better suited to that role than he,' Rough muttered to himself. He would pray about it and turn the situation over in his mind as he did so … once Henry Balnaves had returned he would seek him out for his opinion.

Bearing the Sword of Truth

When Balnaves had returned from the fruitless visit to Henry VIII, John Rough approached him in one of the castle corridors. 'My Lord, may I have a moment of your time. I have something to discuss with you.'

The two men retreated to a corner where John Rough explained to Balnaves how impressed he was with the young tutor, John Knox.

'He has a way with words, you say?' Henry Balnaves exclaimed.

'Yes! You should attend one of his lectures in the chapel on the Gospel of John. I feel that the hand of the Lord is upon him and that you and I should approach him about becoming the preacher and pastor here.'

'You fulfil that role at present, Rough, are you willing to give it up?'

'I will still work as God has need of me, but I am convicted that Knox is the Lord's choice to be the pastor of this town,' John Rough affirmed.

Balnaves held his silence for a moment as he thought on the situation. 'His next lecture is tonight, is that true?' Rough nodded. Henry Balnaves then continued. 'So let us both sit in at the back as he talks and afterwards, if he is as blessed with the spirit of God as you say he is, we shall approach the young man and see what he has to say for himself.'

That night, after John Knox had given another brilliant lecture on the Gospel of John, Henry Balnaves and John Rough sought him out. At the door to the chapel, John Rough put forward his proposal.

'We see a greatness in you, John, that can only be given by God, there is a humility that comes with it. I myself am not the most learned man and you have been such a help to me since you arrived at St Andrews. Where I have struggled to speak against heresy or wrong doctrine, you have given me direction, cleared my thinking and given me courage.'

Balnaves interrupted, 'There are yet people in St Andrews who are not of the Reformed faith and we all know that the believers here need to have sound teaching from the Word of God. You have proven yourself to be a man of God's Word – and with a gift for teaching. I've seen the young men you tutor and many have heard them at their catechism. I know the kind of man you are. Both Rough and I believe that you should take on the role of preacher in this town.'

The colour drained from Knox's face. It was as if he had heard the news of the most dire kind. Rough looked at his friend and was puzzled at his expression.

'John, will you not accept this offer? There is no one better suited to this role.'

John shook his head, 'I will not run where God has not called me.' With that he returned to his lodgings.

Henry Balnaves and John Rough were astonished at the turn of events. 'He said no,' Rough muttered and then louder, 'He said no. Can you believe it? I was so sure …,' he stopped in mid sentence.

Henry scratched his head. 'What do others say about Knox's teaching?'

'I have hardly heard any say a bad word about him in that respect. Some criticise him for being sullen and solemn, but once they have had him at their hearth they soon change their minds. Some say he is too judgemental ... but that is because what he teaches them smarts against their conscience. The greater number of people who hear him rejoice to hear the Word of God preached with passion, a personal plea to the sinner to come to Christ.'

'Well,' Henry declared, 'let's get our heads together and see if we can come up with something to change this situation for the good.'

So that evening, and some evenings thereafter, Rough, Henry Balnaves and one or two others who were of the same mind, set about some godly plotting to see if there was any way they could persuade John Knox to be the preacher in the town of St Andrews.

The following Sunday, John Rough chose what was a very unusual topic for a sermon: 'The Election of Ministers.' It was a long sermon that dealt with the question about how much power a congregation had, even a small one, to request any man to be their minister when they saw in him the necessary gifts of God. He also discussed the great dangers that resulted should that man refuse the request of the congregation.

At the end of Rough's sermon he called out to John Knox, 'Brother, be not offended that I speak to you thus: In the name of God, and of his Son, Jesus

Christ, and in the name of this congregation, I charge you that ye refuse not this holy vocation.'

John Knox was dumbstruck – Rough had taken him totally by surprise.

The preacher turned to the congregation and asked them, 'Was not this your charge to me? And do you not approve this vocation?'

Collectively the congregation replied, 'It was and we approve it.'

The congregation then waited for John's reply, but it was all too much for him. The rugged, sword, wielding bodyguard broke down into copious tears and fled from the chapel to his room to hide himself.

Over the next few days, although John still struggled and was tormented with the path that was laid before him, he knew that accepting this call to the ministry was the right thing to do. 'This calling may lead me to my death like George Wishart, but there are men in this town, in this castle, who have not rejected the heresies of Rome. Preaching the true Word is vital so that the people here will know the truth of God's Word.' John got down on his knees to pray, for he knew he would need God's help.

The following Sunday, Rough sat down in the chapel beside some of the other men who had been instrumental in persuading John to take on the role of preacher.

'They say it is the first time he has preached,' Henry Balnaves whispered to his companion. 'Is that true?'

'Aye, it is,' Rough responded. 'He has lectured, taught, and read the Scriptures in public. He has encouraged others towards a faith in the one true God and in his Son, our Lord Jesus Christ ... but I do believe this is his first attempt at preaching a public sermon. I see some of the university set have come out to hear him,' Rough commented as one or two professors made their way down the aisle. 'There's Major, he was one of Knox's professors when he attended the university. I wonder what message John's chosen to preach on – with all these learned men listening to him?'

At the end of the sermon John Rough and Henry Balnaves took a walk along the ramparts together, looking out to sea. The breakers crashing against the cliffs didn't have the power that John Knox had vocalised that morning in the chapel.

Henry Balnaves took a deep breath of ocean air, 'Those who see themselves with the ecclesiastical power in this town were taken down a peg or two, that's all I can say. Dean Annon was speechless. Knox firmly showed him and us all that sovereignty is with God and not with the Roman Catholic Church.'

Rough nodded his head solemnly, but all he could think of were the ominous words he had overheard as he exited the chapel ... he thought on them privately for a few moments.

'Others have been attacking the branches of the Roman Catholic Church, but today John Knox went for the root. George Wishart never spoke so plainly as he did this morning ... he was burnt at the stake ... it may be that this one will be too.'

Henry looked at his concerned companion and misread his thoughts. 'He's concerned about those troops gathering on the hillside,' Henry Balnaves thought to himself.

'Don't worry about this town, dear friend,' he exclaimed while patting Rough on the back. 'We may seem to be between the devil and the deep blue sea – but I have every hope that our reformed friends in England will soon gather ships and troops to come to our aid. It may be that this siege will not last long in the end.'

Rough grimaced as he remembered the warning Knox had given him not so long ago. 'Don't put your trust in princes nor any man.'

The longer they waited for the promised Somerset and his ships – the more of Mary de Guise's troops gathered on the hill.

Under Siege and Under Sail

One morning, as the sun rose in the sky, a young lad perched on the ramparts of the castle peered into the distance. His call soon echoed down the staircases and corridors. 'Ship ahoy. I've seen sails.'

The year was 1547 and St Andrews had been enjoying a spell of pleasant June weather. The news that sails had been spotted on the horizon sent a thrill of anticipation throughout the crowds holding up inside the Castle.

Mary de Guise's troops had been arriving, steadily, day after day. More captains and commanders, archers and foot soldiers had made encampment outside the town. The castle was a strong fortress, but it could not withstand a siege indefinitely. Their only hope for a victory was to receive help from the sea – but defeat could come from that direction just as easily. Henry Balnaves and others in charge of the defence of the castle raced up to the ramparts to get a better view.

'Is it Somerset at last?' one gasped. Henry could just make out the shape of several ships in the distance – but as yet he could not make out the flags. That would be the only way to tell if these ships were friend or foe.

'It could be the French,' someone whispered urgently.

'Surely not ... if it is they've sailed all the way from Marseilles in very good time. It must be Somerset,' Balnaves willed it to be true.

However, in the distance a flag could be seen unfurling in the wind, on it the gold fleur-de-lys of France glistened in the sunlight. Henry's shoulders visibly sunk as the bad news hit home. This would no longer just be a siege – by the end of the day they would be in a full flung battle.

'Twenty-one galleys,' he muttered, 'all the way from Marseilles. That in itself is unheard of.'

But no one was listening. All around him just stared at the horizon. The enemy had come in great force, at great speed and now they were just a matter of miles from their target.

'Somerset may still come,' one man suggested; sounding more confident than he looked.

'Aye,' another agreed, 'and if not his brother may muster some ships to come to our defence.'

But Knox, who had also joined them, saw the situation for what it was. 'Do not count on these men, they have let you down before.' He turned to Henry Balnaves and told him to prepare for the worst.

Before too long the rebel Reformers were being attacked on every side. Cannon and muskets were in position on the abbey roof. Mary de Guise had her soldiers in a prime position to fire weapons onto the castle. The galleys at sea also attacked from the other side. Everywhere a rebel soldier looked he could see weapons firing on him, or about to fire.

As Knox had predicted, the hoped for help never arrived and as each day passed the rebels defeat became more certain.

Knox looked at the three young lads in his care and wondered what would become of them. He knew that his prospects were either death or slavery on a galley ship … but the lads had some connections that could possibly save their lives. As cannon after cannon rained its shot down on the castle he took the Douglas boys and Alexander aside. 'This battle is not going to go our way. We must accept it. Francis – I'll arrange for one of the lairds in our company to take you out of the town if the opportunity arises. It may be you will yet escape. I am the preacher here and will not leave my people.'

'But when the Castle surrenders,' Francis argued, 'that will mean you'll be for the gallows or the galleys.'

Knox could see the lads were anxious, 'Do not worry, boys. Such an outcome will not be for you. You are all from noble families. If you are still here when the battle is lost, I do not believe you will spend long in prison. If the escape goes to plan or once you are released, Alexander, you'll go with the Douglas boys to their aunt's in the country. It may be that your fathers will be able to get word to you there.'

'Mr Knox? What will happen to you? I don't want you to die,' the youngest Douglas boy pleaded.

Knox reached out a hand and ruffled the lad's hair, 'Don't you worry about that, young sir. The Lord will look after me. He even cares for the birds of the air, or the lion's cubs that are hungry … I am in his care and want to be nowhere else.'

After two months of siege and fighting, with a plague thrown in for good measure, the rebels surrendered to the combined forces of the French and Mary de Guise. In the chaos that ensued after the surrender, Knox was separated from his young students. He didn't see them on the ship and hoped fervently that they had managed some escape, although he wasn't certain.

A treaty of sorts had been signed and it seemed that once they arrived in France, the captives would be released and allowed to live a life of freedom there. However, when they arrived in France the terms of this treaty were broken.

The noblemen were imprisoned. Knox, being of a lower rank, wasn't even allowed to land on French soil. He and the other low ranking captives from St Andrews would spend the rest of their sentence as galley-slaves for the French. They would be the manpower that would propel the ship across the seas.

Huddled with other men on board, Knox looked at the wooden galley that would be the centre of his existence for many months to come. A young man who had been a guard at St Andrews stood beside him as they waited to be chained to their oars.

'What's the name of this vessel?' he asked anxiously.

'Notre Dame,' John muttered between clenched teeth. He turned to the young man and looked him in the eye, 'Be under no illusion, lad – you are now a slave. They'll try to bend your back and your will on this ship. The food you will eat will be the barest rations – enough to keep your body and soul together, but no more. Take a look about you – you will have no privacy. Can you see any place for you to relieve yourself even? Take care, if you can, for your cleanliness, for without it you will suffer disease because of your own filth and the filth of others. We're easy targets for any cannon that we sail too close to. If the English navy don't get us, it will either be storm or pestilence.' The prospects were pretty poor.

John looked at the bright blue French sky. There were some months of good weather still ahead of them before the winter arrived. That meant several months of hard rowing as he and the other men put their backs against the sea. If it was calm they would row to get the ship to move a few feet across the water. If it was stormy they would row to avoid crashing against the rocks. Then there would still be times when extra speed was needed. John knew that as galley-slaves in a French ship they were at risk of being shot at by the enemies of France ... the same English troops that they had pleaded to help them at St Andrews, and who it was now rumoured, were marching towards that city several weeks too late.

But there was no point in dwelling on that turn of events. This was where God had placed him, on board a French vessel with one hundred and fifty captives, thieves and fraudsters. With whips on their backs they would row and row until the winter made it impossible to sail. Galley-slaves were easily replaceable so he did not expect much in the way of bodily care or comfort as they criss-crossed the oceans. Their French captors would hopefully not whip them too hard or too often

– but John knew that he would certainly feel the cut of the cord as it cracked his flesh.

The young man beside him asked another question, 'Do we know how long we will be on this ship? I don't remember them saying anything about when we'll be released.'

John laughed quietly, 'You're right. They said nothing about that.'

The young man's face fell as he began to realise how hard his life would now be – and that there was virtually no prospect of freedom.

The ship itself was between 100 and 150 feet (30.48 and 45.72 metres) long and 30 feet (9.144 metres) wide. But it stood only 6 feet (1.8288 metres) above the water line. That was what made it unsuitable for sailing in heavy seas. The ship held 150 galley-slaves and there were six to each oar with 25 oars in each boat. The oars were 45 feet (13.716 metres) long and passed through the sides of the ship. The rowers were kept chained to their oar if they were not doing any other duties. Each slave was given a basic uniform that consisted of a coarse brown tunic, a vest, two shirts, two sets of breeches and a red cap. However, shoes were only issued if the slave had duties to perform on shore.

All these items were handed to Knox by a French sailor. Dressing quickly, the last item he put on was the red cap. 'I don't expect to keep this garment for much longer,' he mused. 'A good gust of wind will soon swipe this off my head.' His spare breeches and shirt were tied up in a rough piece of sacking and laid out in the hold underneath the deck in a corner where he hoped to have some sleep ... soon. But all thoughts of sleep were soon banished as the ship's captain came on board. John was quickly chained to an oar with five other men – soon they were heaving their bodies back and forward, back and forward slowly urging the ship out into the English Channel.

The young guardsman, who had spoken to John earlier, looked as though he was going to ask another question. John told him to save his breath, shut his mouth and row.

Life on board the galley ship was tough. The French sailors did not put up with any slacking. If it looked as though one oar wasn't pulling its weight, all the men on that oar would feel the sting of the whip as it lashed across their backs. There was at least a rota in place which meant the rowing was done in shifts of which there was three. So if you weren't rowing, you would be mending sails or nets. If you weren't working on the deck, you would be in the hold eating or sleeping.

As the good summer weather drew to an end, John felt the change. The wind increased and there was a cruel bite to it when you were on deck. A taste of ice and snow was on the air. 'I'll be glad when we change course for a warmer climate,' he muttered to his young friend.

The young man smiled. His skin was weather-beaten now, his face covered in a shaggy beard. The skinny youngster that had joined the galleon in France, had grown into a man despite his poor rations and bad conditions. He turned to John and patted him on the back as they were released from their chains and given leave to go below. 'I can't believe what I'm hearing,' he exclaimed. 'Is John Knox saying that he is looking forward to returning to France?'

John nodded. 'Aye, France. I can hardly believe that I've said it myself.'

'Do you think rations will be better on shore than on ship?' one of the other captives asked.

'Better than ship's biscuit?' another exclaimed. 'Is there anything better than ship's biscuit?'

The men laughed when another interrupted with the sarcastic comment, 'Don't forget watery soup three times a week. Yum, yum!'

Two days later the order was given to turn the ship south, towards France. There would be no more sailing now until the better weather arrived.

Let the Lady Swim!

Not long after John and the other galley-slaves disembarked, they were put behind bars. Being in a French jail was not an enjoyable experience, but the few short weeks on shore would be a relief. John had begun to fail physically and he wondered if another season at sea would be the end of him.

When the spring returned, the men were taken once again to the galley ship and chained to their oars before setting out to sea. Knox found himself taking on the role of preacher and pastor once more. The men looked to him for encouragement, guidance and prayer.

It was the custom of the French crew to attend the Mass – a Roman Catholic practice where the bread was believed to actually turn into the body of Christ and the wine turn into his blood. This was a heresy that Knox hated with a passion. Many of the Scots on board agreed with him and whenever they were forced to listen to the Mass on shore or on board the ship, they would cover their ears with their caps. John was relieved that the little red cap had not blown off in the North Sea as he had predicted. 'It does have its uses,' he admitted to himself as he grabbed it round his ears while yet another Roman Catholic priest recited the Mass to the captured Scots.

When in port one day, the lieutenant of the ship thought it would be amusing to bring on board the ship a painted image of the Virgin Mary. They wanted to force the Scots slaves to worship the image. Knox was the first to have the idol forced between his manacled hands. They knew that if Knox caved in the other men would too – if he didn't they had the perfect excuse to beat him.

Knox stood there with the painted image in his grasp – and straightaway took his chance. With a great heave he threw the painted statue into the air. The French gasped in horror and the Scots slaves laughed in astonishment as the statue sailed over the side of the ship and was heard to splash as it hit the water. Knox called out as it went under, 'Let "Our Lady" save herself – she is light enough, let her swim!'

A desperate flurry of sailors and lieutenants rushed to the side of the ship, hoping to rescue their cherished idol from the waves.

That night, as the ship was tossed about in a blustery gale, John was asked why he'd done it.

'Your back will smart for weeks after the beating they gave you,' one man admonished him.

'I care not for my back, but for the one true, living God, who should share his glory with no other and certainly not a gaudy, painted lady like that one.'

'Did they manage to fish her out?' another asked.

'There's no sign of the dame,' one young man piped up. 'But I've just heard the captain tear some strips off that lieutenant. He's ordered him to leave those Scots "to their own godless" ways.'

John smiled, relieved and thankful. 'I'll not have to bother with those idols again,' he exclaimed.

That spring their travels took the galley ship back to the North Sea. Fighting between Mary de Guise and the English had stopped for the winter, but now that the fair weather had returned, the sound of steel against steel echoed around the disputed Scottish territory once again. In fact, as John Knox put his back to a forty-five foot oar his home town of Haddington was taken and plundered by English forces. The prophecy of George Wishart had come true. In answer to an urgent plea from Mary de Guise the French King sent 140 vessels to her aid, amongst those were twenty-six galley ships – one of which was the vessel John Knox was helping to row.

Below deck and out of sight of their French captors, the Scots galley-slaves urgently discussed if there was any way they could escape. But of course there was no such opportunity. 'We're chained to our oars whenever we're on board. Below deck it's impossible to get past the guards.'

'But isn't there something we can do? We're rowing these ships to fight against our friends and country-men. Those who weren't captured at St Andrews have joined forces with the English against Mary de Guise. These are the men the French soldiers on board this vessel are going to fight. And it's not just a matter of country against country this time. Our friends and families in Scotland are fighting for the freedom to worship God, to follow the true faith. And here we are bringing people to their shore who would trample on that freedom and on the true faith.'

John shook his head. What could he say? A friend looked across at him, concerned at his unusual silence. 'John, are you well?' he asked. Again John said nothing. 'Feel his head someone. I don't like the look of this.'

'What do you mean, Balfour?' one of the other men asked.

'Look at him, man, can you not see that he is suffering from a fever? Call the ship's surgeon, have him take a look at him.'

Just then Knox suddenly collapsed on the wooden floor, quite unconscious.

Some days passed while John remained delirious below deck. His friends took it in turns to see to his needs, but they despaired for his life as his fever grew worse, rather than better. Early one evening, David Balfour, the one who had spotted his fever in the first place, knelt down by John's side. 'I can see the shores of Scotland in the distance, John. Although we're captives, we're nearly home.'

Something in John's eyes seemed to change as he heard those words. David called over to one of the other men. 'Quick, I'm going to try something. Help me carry him to the deck – just to the opening hatch. I'm sure they'll let us give him some fresh air.'

Struggling to carry the sick man up the ladder, they eventually managed to get John's exhausted body to a point where he too could see the cliffs of the east coast of Scotland.

Closer and closer they came to the land of his birth. David Balfour raised him up a bit more so that he could see just a bit further, 'Do you recognise anything, John?' he asked.

Somehow John gathered the strength to raise his head and in the distance he saw Fife and the spires of St Andrews. 'Yes,' he whispered at last. 'I know it well, for I see the steeple of that place where God first, in public, opened my mouth to his glory.'

These were the first words Knox had spoken in many days ... and then he spoke again, only this time much clearer and with the old determination that his friends knew so well. 'I am fully persuaded, how weak that ever I now appear, that I shall not depart this life till my tongue shall glorify his godly name in the same place.'

Finally, after the battles were over and another winter was about to begin, the French fleet returned to the shelter of ports and harbours. John was still seriously weak – but with no further rowing required until the better weather returned he could at least rest while repairing sails for the next bout of rowing in the spring.

In the thick of winter, the galley-slaves had some measure of excitement. Secret messages had been smuggled into the prison, which told of how some of the Scottish lairds were planning an escape from their prison on St Michael. They wanted to ask John if he thought it was right of them to try this – and John agreed. 'Write this,' he dictated to one of his friends.

'They can take every chance for their freedom as long as there is no blood spilt ... to that I could never consent.'

The reply was smuggled out the way the previous letter had been smuggled in. But bad news filtered back. 'The French lad who smuggled in the letter has betrayed the lairds. He has stolen their money and informed on them to the enemy. They haven't been arrested – but have had to separate in order to get back to England.'

'When will we hear if they've made it or not?' one man asked.

'It could be months, maybe even as long as a year,' John replied, 'before we hear if they are alive or dead.'

Free at Last!

But it wasn't that long before John heard some news about freedom ... not just about the lairds' freedom but also about his own. In the background, the wheels of power had been turning and an exchange of prisoners was arranged. So in the early months of 1549 John found himself in England, during the reign of Edward VI, Henry VIII's only son.

Henry Balnaves met John as he set foot on English soil, 'Welcome, John, welcome. I never thought I would see this day. You and I free at last. And what plans I have for you, Mr Knox. But first you are to come to my lodgings at court, for there I have fine food to feed you with and fresh clothes to replace these rags – and then we'll have plenty time to talk about how I am going to introduce you to the young king!'

John stood transfixed on the quayside – astonished at what he had just heard. In what seemed like a whirlwind, John was soon fed, washed, clothed and a few days later he was standing before the ruler of the realm – the young King Edward. In the year 1547, Edward had been crowned king when he was only nine years old. A delicate young boy, but he had, however, a steely nature, inherited from his Tudor father – and he had a firm Protestant faith. Knox was very impressed with his king – not for his power or prestige, but for his maturity and intelligence, and for the godly witness the young man was to his subjects.

'Reformers are welcomed to preach everywhere,' John exclaimed as he and Henry Balnaves returned from the throne room. 'And now the king himself has given me a congregation in Berwick.'

'You'll be well suited there, John,' Balnaves exclaimed as he mounted his horse. 'It's a border town – and you coming from Haddington will be familiar with their ways. Berwick has changed hands several times as your home town has too. It has, I'm afraid, a rather unruly garrison of over six hundred soldiers. But you're well able to cope with that, I'm sure.'

John grimaced slightly as he mounted his horse. 'I have heard that there is much stealing and violence in that town. There is bad feeling between the townsfolk and those who find themselves wounded and homeless because of the fighting.'

Henry nodded. 'Yes. It's a troubled place. There is bitterness there and hatred. Although England is Protestant under the young king – the North has always been Roman Catholic. That is where their loyalties still lie.'

Henry nudged the flank of his horse to pick up the pace a bit. 'Come now, John, let's get our minds onto more practical things. What do you think you'll need once you get there?'

'Well, I have nothing,' John replied.

'Let's start there,' Henry called out as he galloped off, John following close behind.

The provisions John gathered over the next few days were enough to be carried on the backs of a couple of sturdy horses. Having been a slave on a galley ship, he had arrived in England with just what he had on his back – which was very poor provision indeed. Now, fully clothed and with his own horse, he was packing more food and cloth than he had seen in years. Books too found their way into his satchels. Quills and paper for the writing he hoped to do.

Henry waved goodbye to his friend as he set off for the North. 'Write to me soon, John. I look forward to hearing how the Lord is at work in Berwick.'

It wasn't long before Henry Balnaves heard good things about John Knox and Berwick so that during one of his meetings with King Edward, he had a favourable report to give of his friend.

'Your Majesty will be delighted to hear of Mr Knox's work in the North.'

'Indeed, I am most interested in this Scottish preacher of ours. Pray continue.'

'He has performed wonders in Berwick. In a comparatively short time, that lawless town has discovered peace and unity. Before Knox's arrival in Berwick, it was notorious for its violence. Soldiers would fight each other to the death, in full view of the public … yet nothing was done to install justice or order. Now, since John Knox's arrival, the town has become an example of quietness and good manners. God has so blessed his Word and the labours of Mr Knox, that I would recommend that town as a dwelling place for any family or friend.'

'The Christians there, Your Majesty, report to me a great joy in hearing Knox preach the Word. Both Scots and English eat the Lord's Supper together. They eat the bread and drink the wine in remembrance of our Lord Jesus Christ – free of Roman Catholic traditions.

'Knox has also started to write a treatise on prayer. I've copied out a few lines from his recent letter, where he has gathered together some of his thoughts.'

The young king leaned forward eagerly. His thirst for God's Word and godly teaching was clearly seen in his enthusiasm.

> *Prayer is an earnest and familiar talking with God, to whom we declare our miseries, whose support and help we implore and desire in our adversities, and whom we laud and praise for our benefits received .... Let no man think himself unworthy to call and pray to God, because he hath grievously offended his majesty in times past; but let him bring to God a sorrowful and repenting heart, saying with David, 'Heal my soul, O Lord, for I have offended against thee. Before I was afflicted, I transgressed; but now let me observe thy commandments.*

'Yes,' Edward nodded his head solemnly. 'That passage is based on Psalm 6, I believe. Knox is a man of God and one that I am pleased to have preaching in my realm. Keep me informed of his progress Balnaves,' Edward called out as the courtier retreated from the throne room.

Over the next few months, correspondence regularly made its way from Berwick to London. The letters didn't just come from Knox, but from other contacts that Henry Balnaves had in the northern territories.

'I'm hearing more about the Bowes family these days,' he commented to an acquaintance. 'Knox has mentioned them too. If I didn't know Knox better, I'd be tempted to believe there is a courtship taking place.'

'What?' exclaimed Henry's companion. 'Knox is too much of a bachelor to spend time in sweet-talking women.'

Balnaves laughed out loud. 'You're right. And besides, Knox is too busy with his preaching to go courting. Judging by his last letter, he has been extra busy lately ... the bishop summoned him to preach in public at Newcastle in order to speak up for that pamphlet he wrote against the Mass. Which reminds me, Knox sent me a letter. I'm wondering if it might be suitable to read out to the king. Now, where did I leave it?'

Henry leafed through some papers on his desk and then came across the last few pages of John's letter. 'Let's hope it's not too controversial,' Henry murmured. 'Hmmm ... here's something ...'

Who has burdened us with all these ceremonies, fasting ... unlawful vows and the idolatry of the Mass? ... In the papist Mass the priests are placed by themselves at one altar and they must be clad in clothes that are not mentioned in the New Testament.

Is this necessary that things be done decently in order? Dare they say that the supper of Jesus Christ was done without order and indecently when they did not wear such vestments? In the supper of the Lord, the bread was broken, the cup distributed amongst all according to God's holy commandment. In the Mass the congregation get nothing except to look at joukings, noddings, crossings, turnings, upliftings which are nothing but a diabolical profanation of Christ's supper. Now jouk, nod, cross as ye wish – but they are your own inventions ... Jesus Christ said, 'Eat, of this, and drink of this, all do this in remembrance of Me.' Christ commands us not to gaze upon it, bow, jouk and beck thereto – but we are to eat and drink of it ourselves. We are not to look at others doing this – unless we would confess that the death of Christ means nothing to us.

Henry, the astute politician that he was, wondered if perhaps this part of Knox's letter was just a little too inflammatory for the English king .... 'I'll leave it till later,' he decided.

But if Henry was an astute politician he was perhaps not such a good judge of human nature as he thought he was. He had dismissed any possibility of a romance ... when in fact John Knox was indeed quietly courting a young woman named Marjorie Bowes.

Marriage and Monsters

One Lord's Day in Berwick, Mrs Bowes and her daughter had come to hear Knox preach. It was the start of two long lasting relationships. One between a husband and wife and one between a preacher and a penitent sinner – for Mrs Bowes was a woman under great spiritual stress. Uncertain of her own salvation, she soon became a firm supporter of Knox and the Reformed faith ... even against her husband's wishes.

When Henry Balnaves received news of Knox's marriage to Marjorie he was astonished. 'I can't believe it, but I must,' he exclaimed, 'for it is here in black and white on this parchment. Though for a wedding to take place without the consent of any of the bride's male relatives is practically unheard of.'

This is exactly what had happened. One quiet afternoon, in a secret ceremony somewhere in the North of England, Marjorie Bowes was given in marriage to the Scottish preacher, John Knox.

'Your life won't be easy,' Knox sighed as he held the hand of his young wife.

'I know,' she said, smiling gently.

But she couldn't have known the difficulties that persecution would bring her and her husband. Her life wouldn't be easy – the fight for the Reformation would be long and hard.

After two years had passed in Berwick it was time for John and Marjorie to move on – to Newcastle. While he was there Knox received another appointment – Chaplain to the King. He still preached in the North but there would be times when the king would summon him to preach at court.

Some thought it a strange appointment for a man who was so well known for speaking his mind. Knox had spoken out against the king's decision to imprison his Uncle Somerset in the Tower of London. That outspokenness itself could have turned the king against Knox, but it didn't. There was something about John Knox that appealed to the young monarch. Perhaps he saw in this Scottish preacher a measure of integrity that was lacking in all the other courtiers around him. Many stood up forcefully for the Protestant faith – yet if you scratched at the surface these men would have revealed a different nature entirely. Well-known courtiers like Dudley and even Marjorie's father, Mr Bowes, would have changed their faith at the drop of a hat, if the circumstances had been different and Edward's sister, Mary, had been on the throne. Edward, however, saw in Knox a man of truth.

Some accused the young king of being merciless when eventually he sent his uncle to the executioner. John Knox, however, knew that the king could not be blamed. 'He is not master of his own will,' he explained to his wife. 'There are plenty schemers who are influencing him for their own ends … and these men are ruthless. The young man knows not who to trust and who can blame him.'

Marjorie took a long look at her husband's face. 'Lord Dudley will escort you to London shortly to preach in the presence of the king ... he is one that you doubt, is he not?'

'Aye,' Knox said solemnly. 'I do not trust that man. He wanted to have me as Bishop in Rochester ... but I refused. The king may have requested it but it was Dudley's idea.'

'Why did Dudley want you to be Bishop of Rochester?' Marjorie asked quietly.

'I think he would rather have me out of the North. Here, I have been preaching with God's grace and men have been listening. Dudley hates the way I preach against the Mass and perhaps he influences the king on this matter too.'

'I fear that you have made Dudley your enemy,' Marjorie suggested awkwardly.

'That is not my concern,' Knox muttered. 'That man will soon tire of trying to catch me out.'

Marjorie's worry lines disappeared at her husband's gruff humour. 'Your congregation in Newcastle and the people in Berwick will miss you when you are at your work in London.'

John nodded solemnly. 'Yes, that is what I am really concerned over ... the people of God and their need for the preaching of God's Word. But the young king and his court have need of that too. If God spares me I can do both.'

After his arrival in London he wrote his congregation a letter to calm their fears. 'Be not moved with every wind of doctrine ... do not doubt the virtue of that religion preached amongst you by a wretched, weak and most feeble man ... to this gospel stick fast brethren.'

The royal court, however, was not somewhere that John relished. Many had their heads turned by the fact that they were in the king's service ... but not Knox. John could see that the men who sought the king's favour were rotten to the core. He knew of men who were committing adultery in secret and in public. John longed to get back to the North to be with his wife and his own congregation. That Christmas he got his wish.

After a particularly rousing sermon on Christmas Day, there were some quiet mutterings amongst the congregation. 'Knox might regret the words he spoke,' a man suggested. 'There was more than one powerful noble in the congregation who he riled.'

And that was true. John wasn't making friends or influencing people for his own good – he simply spoke the truth and forcefully at that. Shortly after that Christmas Day service, John was accused of treason and summoned to appear before Lord Wharton. He scribbled a note to his wife before he was taken away ... not knowing if these would be the last words he would ever share with her.

However, if Knox had enemies he had friends too – and they were in high places. Knox's enemies had forgotten that he had one particularly important friend – the king.

Although the monarch was weak and sickly, he was still the highest in the land. As a result, John was released without charge and allowed to return to the North ... but the stress of the trial had brought on John Knox a sickness that involved a sore stomach and severe headaches. He arrived home with a pale look across his face.

'Husband,' Marjorie called out as she ran to meet him. 'What is wrong? Are you ill?' she called out in concern. 'What ails you?'

'I am not well, that is true,' John muttered as he sat down at their fireside. 'But it is not that which troubles me ...,' he turned to speak to his wife, but she was no longer there. The sounds from the back of the house told him she was frantically making some food, giving the maid orders to light the fire in the bedroom, to fetch the doctor .... 'I'll not tell her my real concern,' John thought to himself. 'I fear it is not I who will be dead before the year is out ... but the young king.' John sighed. 'However, I will not speak of it for it is treason to speak of the death of a king ... even such a sick one as this.'

The king's sickness became a sickness that lead to death – and to a great constitutional crisis in the land. King Henry had sired two daughters and one son – to three different women. The daughters were Mary, daughter of Catherine of Aragon – Henry's first wife; and Elizabeth, daughter of Anne Boleyn – his second wife, the woman he had divorced his first wife for. His daughter, Mary, had been named as illegitimate as had his daughter, Elizabeth, after her mother's execution for treason. But before Henry's death both girls had been reinstated as heirs to the throne. There was one problem though … Mary, the next heir to the throne after Edward was an obsessively loyal Roman Catholic. As her brother, Edward, lay dying he and his immediate courtiers had a decision to make. Was the country to be left in the hands of his sister, Mary, and her Catholic supporters? Should the throne not be given to his other sister, Elizabeth, who was more supportive of the Protestants?

A surprise decision was made by Edward as the throne was left to a young cousin – Lady Jane Grey. When Edward's sister, Mary, finally regained power she looked on the act as treason – and Lady Jane Grey was executed after being queen for only nine days.

The situation for reformers across the land was dire.

Knox had to, once again, flee for his life. Leaving his wife behind him in Berwick, he smuggled himself on board a ship that would take him to a country that he had been to once before … France.

Though John was distressed to leave his wife behind, he hadn't left her completely alone. Her mother was now living with her. Mr Bowes had made his wife's life so intolerable, she had left him to come to the home of her daughter and son-in-law. 'It's not a good witness to have husbands and wives behaving like this … but she had nowhere else to go. And Marjorie can look after her and she can look after Marjorie. Though I'd rather look after my own wife,' John muttered as his ship drew near the quayside of Dieppe.

On arrival, John pushed his way through all the merchants, traders and visitors. He wasn't one of them – he was a refugee, full of doubts and guilt. 'Should I have stayed to suffer with my people? Am I not like one of those faint-hearted lads who run at the first sign of battle? I pray to God that I will be restored to the front lines of this fight once more.'

Over the coming weeks and months, news would trickle through from England of yet another preacher thrown into the Tower of London or burned at the stake … Cranmer, Latimer, Ridley, Hooper, Bradford. Ordinary men and women found themselves tortured, imprisoned and put to death because of their refusal to give up their faith in Christ. The Roman Catholic Church that worshipped saints and relics, statues and icons forced many to turn back to the old idolatrous ways … but a great number of the Reformed faith remained true, despite the pressure to convert.

John often wrote to his congregations at home, or to some pastor whom he had heard was under threat of his life. 'Keep the faith,' he urged.

> *Do not recant and go back to the idolatry of Rome because of your fear. For, if you do, what will you leave to your children? Cling to the plain truth of God's Word. God's revelation is not given twice. Look at those countries where the apostles once preached – in Israel; Asia; Africa – what of these places now? There is only ignorance and false sects. What we are seeing in our own nation now is a national judgment for our national sin.*

One thing that Knox debated during this time was whether or not Scotland and England were in such trouble, due to the fact that women were on the thrones.

These two countries were being ruled by Mary de Guise and Mary Tudor – and both were Roman Catholics. In Knox's time it was unusual for women to receive such high honours. And certainly these two women had done nothing to deserve such advantages. Mary de Guise was not even a queen, but she ruled as one and an evil one at that. Mary Tudor may have been the heir to the throne … but she shamefully used her power in ill ways.

So we can see that Knox's complaint about the female monarchs was not about their gender, but about their godless lives; and their ruthless natures. Both rulers were cruel to many of their subjects and deliberately persecuted the Reformed church. Honest citizens, whose only crime was to worship outside the Roman Catholic Church, were punished and killed.

Knox, who had had the privilege of serving a loving and faithful young king – could not help but see the contrast between that monarch and the two women who now ruled. It broke his heart to see the two lands so abused by the monstrous regiment of women.

It was during this time, as a refugee on the continent, that Knox made his first journey to Geneva and met the Reformer, John Calvin. From that day, Calvin became a respected friend and mentor of Knox –one who he would regularly consult. They didn't always agree, far from it. John Knox was a bit too revolutionary for John Calvin, a bit too eager to fight. But if it was an issue of theology, religion, Christian practice, personal advice – John Knox would seek out John Calvin for guidance and by and large they would come to a mutual understanding.

One day, Knox approached Calvin about a request he had received.

'Let me see it, John,' Calvin reached out for the letter.

'It's from some of the English refugees who have settled in Frankfurt-am-Maine in Germany. They have been given the use of a building and have asked me to become one of their three pastors. I have been thinking and praying about this, yet still I'm not sure what answer I should give ... that's why I'm consulting you. I respect your wisdom and spiritual insight. What do you think I should do?'

Calvin didn't need much time to consider the letter.

'Dear brother,' he exclaimed. 'You should go – the flock of Christ needs you.'

So John left, but it wasn't long before he was back in Geneva. Calvin shook his head as he heard Knox recount the stories of division, heresy and discord that had crept into the church.

'There were troublemakers there,' Knox sighed. 'They did all they could to stir up dispute and then they stopped me preaching, accused me of treason against the Emperor and even refused me entry to the church building to worship. I had to return to Geneva. I could have just given in, to preserve unity, but I have been urging others in more dangerous places to cling to the Word of God, to stand firm at all costs. I had to leave – and a small number, perhaps fifty, have come with me.'

'More believers for our flock in Geneva then,' Calvin declared. 'But the outcome of this situation is that you are now no longer part of the English church, is that right?'

John nodded solemnly. 'I have no home and I have no church.'

'For the moment then content yourself with Geneva, some study and my friendship. This may be a period of rest for you, one that you can put to good use.'

John nodded, if only his wife were with him, he would be more than content … but Marjorie was in the land of Mary Tudor, the wife of a well-known runaway reformer and far from safe.

Which was why six months later, in response to an urgent plea from Mrs Bowes, John Knox left Geneva on a rescue mission to fetch Marjorie and her mother to the freedom and safety of Geneva. 'I can't leave them in Roman Catholic England while I relax in safety here.'

What John didn't realise, was that in the eight years since he had left Scotland, he had become a bit of a hero, famous even. When he arrived back in Berwick, trying to attract as little notice as possible, the news on the streets was not what he had expected.

The Return

'Something's afoot in Scotland, it seems,' John said as he absorbed every word from the letter that had just arrived from Edinburgh. 'I know your mother is set on me taking you both back to Geneva ... but what if God wants me to return to Scotland?'

'If that is God's will it should be your will and mine and my mother's,' Marjorie stated emphatically.

Knox smiled ... his wife had accepted on their wedding day that life with her new husband would not be easy. Maybe she hadn't known exactly what she had been letting herself in for ... but she was a godly young woman and a constant support to her husband. 'If you go to Scotland,' she said quietly. 'I know that I'll not be able to come with you.'

'It would be impossible,' Knox said. 'Well, it would certainly be foolishness.' Holding her close, he whispered a prayer for her safety and God's protection over them both until they met again. 'God willing we shall meet again, my love.'

Marjorie nodded in agreement, a transparent tear trickling down her pale face. 'Mother wants to speak with you about a doctrine she has had trouble with lately. She has been depressed in spirits again. Could you bring her some comfort from God's Word? She is always better when she has had good preaching.'

'Yes, your mother is a godly woman, but sorely troubled with doubts and fears.'

'She needs a good pastor,' Marjorie added.

With that, Knox went through to the fireplace to speak with his mother-in-law. What would it be tonight? Assurance, perhaps? 'Am I really one of the Lord's redeemed?' It was often an issue that troubled her. Thankfully, the gospel was simple and direct. When it wasn't dressed up in the fancy falsehoods of Catholicism it was a message that the simple and the great of the land could understand. It was just that Marjorie's mother needed constant reminding of this. Thankfully, Knox was more than willing to open the warm, living Word of God on such a cold night as this.

John sat down beside her and began to speak. 'Our Lord and Saviour, Jesus Christ, came to save the ungodly. Salvation is a gift, not something that we can earn or pay for.'

Mrs Bowes nodded her head, relieved to have the preacher back in the home.

A couple of weeks later, Knox secretly sneaked over the border and took refuge in the house of John Syme in Edinburgh. Taking him in the back door, where a young Scots lass was scrubbing floors, Mr Syme was in a bit of a fluster. 'I can hardly believe it's you, Mr Knox. It's such an honour to have you in my house. Watch the bucket,' he said sharply to the young servant. But she didn't seem to notice as she was simply staring at the man before her.

'Is it really him?' she whispered.

'Yes,' Mr Syme smiled. 'It really is!'

Knox looked on quite confused. 'Does that lass even know who I am?'

'Know who you are? Of course the lassie knows who you are! You're John Knox. You're a legend in your own time.'

John tried to cover a snort of laughter. But Mr Syme assumed that his guest had caught a cold and quickly ordered the young maid to fetch some warm water for Mr Knox to wash himself and to make sure there was a roaring fire in the front room.

That night, as John was reintroduced to the land of his birth through the conversation of his host, the rumour that Knox was back spread like wildfire through the narrow streets, closes and alleyways of the city.

When Knox agreed to speak the following day, he arrived at the venue to a massive crowd, eager to hear one of their own speak. The people arrived from every nook and cranny of the capital. Knox praised God as he looked at the people before him. 'To think that I wasn't even sure if leaving Geneva was the right decision ... but now when I see my own people so eager to hear the true Word of God, it warms my heart. May God grant them their heart's desire – himself.'

After the meeting, John talked again with Mr Syme. 'The people here are more than ready to throw off the baggage of Rome,' John exclaimed. 'It astonishes me, for it was not like this eight years ago.'

'You are right. The land has changed and is changing still. Tomorrow, you leave for Angus to preach to the people in the farming communities there. I believe you will meet with some old friends.'

John smiled, 'Lord Burnstane will be one. The last I saw of him, he had made his escape out of a window and was fleeing from Lord Bothwell's troops.'

Other memories of that night wiped the smile of Knox's face. It was easy to allow the thrill and excitement of the last few days to dull his wits and hide the fact that he was still in danger. The common people may have tired of the Mass and the deadness of the Roman Catholic Church – but those in power were a different matter altogether. This was still the land that had martyred George Wishart.

As Knox travelled from town to town, speaking to the common man and the high-born lairds, news of this travelling preacher even came to the ears of the Regent – Mary de Guise. 'Who is this man?' she asked.

'Knox,' a bishop bitterly replied. 'He is just a common little heretic that the people are flocking to.'

'What should we do about him?' Mary de Guise demanded.

So the first of many plots were hatched and Knox was accused of heresy. The clergy demanded that he come and answer those charges in Edinburgh. To their surprise, Knox agreed. The clergy panicked and quickly withdrew their charges. Knox's fame had gone before him and they had no wish to cross swords with this sharp Scot. His words were his weapons and he would destroy them.

Knox's preaching was like a trumpet blast echoing around the land. Knox felt great things were going to happen in the land. The confidence of the reformers grew and they even found themselves thinking that perhaps Mary de Guise would let them worship in freedom. They wrote her a letter, hoping that she 'would listen to the heart cry of her people.'

Mary de Guise received the letter, but when she read it she just treated it like a joke.

'Is it April First?' she asked one of her bishops. 'This letter is certainly from a fool.'

When John Knox heard what she had said, he was crushed. 'Why did I expect her, of all people, to agree to our requests?'

The glorious days of confidence and excitement seemed to be coming to an end. All hopes of a national Protestant church of Scotland were vanquished. Over the border in England, Mary Tudor increased her persecution. Mary de Guise still had French troops who would jump to her call at a moment's notice. It was at that point that John Knox received a call from Geneva. 'The English church there want me to be their pastor,' he told some of his friends as they sat solemnly musing on what might have been. 'I've decided to return. Our plans here have come to nothing. I've made arrangements to send Marjorie and her mother on ahead of me … but I leave you all here with a sore heart.'

Which is why he wrote to them from Geneva, to tell them of his love and to encourage them in the faith.

Beloved brethren, ye are God's creatures and formed to his own image … it was for your redemption that the most precious blood of the beloved Son of God was shed. It is to you that he has commanded his gospel and glad tidings to be preached; and it is for you he has prepared the heavenly inheritance ... and it is at this point I say, 'All men are created equal' ... God requires of rich and poor the same duty for the same benefits. For the prince he demands that he refuse himself and follow Christ − of the poor man he desires the same. God requires those who are noble and those who are of low estate to believe in their heart and with their mouth to confess that Jesus Christ is the only saviour of the World.

But again his time in Geneva was short-lived ... Once again a call came to him from Scotland.

'Scotland?' Marjorie gasped. 'They want you back?'

'Yes, look, Glencairn, James Stewart, Erskine and Lorne have signed it.'

Marjorie took the letter and looked at the impressive list of noble names. James Stewart was the half-brother of the young Queen Mary.

'And you plan to go?'

'Not just yet, I'm not sure if the time is right and I would prefer to have more news from Scotland before I make a final decision.'

But three months later, John was making the dangerous trek through the hostile country of France. Persecution seemed to be everywhere in Europe and as Knox arrived in Dieppe, news of deaths from Mary Tudor's England came daily. John Rough had been one of them − burned at the stake at Smithfield. 'How was he there?' Knox asked one of the French believers. 'I thought he had been living abroad.'

'That is true, but he made a visit to England and it was while he was there he was persuaded to preach for a congregation of a martyred pastor. It wasn't long before he was martyred too.'

John Knox sighed at the death of another friend, one who had been responsible for persuading him to preach. Now here he was in Dieppe, waiting for instructions from Scotland that did not seem to be coming.

Imagine John's disappointment when two letters arrived from Scotland – one saying 'Maybe you shouldn't come' and another saying, 'You definitely shouldn't come.'

It seemed that the people who had so eagerly asked him to return to Scotland were now getting cold feet. Some of the Lords felt that perhaps Mary de Guise was warming to them.

Knox wrote back expressing his disappointment and urging them to accept their duty as noblemen of the realm. 'Being a true nobleman is not about title, birth, name or lands, but rather about defending the oppressed even at risk of your own lives. The Lord can raise up leaders even from the very dung-hill!'

While keeping occupied in Dieppe by preaching to the small number of French Protestants there, John was kept informed about the situation in Scotland. The news was that Mary de Guise was on the brink of having her most dearest wish granted. Her daughter, who was being brought up in the French court, was soon to be married to the Dauphin, the heir to the throne of France. The marriage contract stated that on the wedding day the Crown Matrimonial would be offered, which meant that the heir to the throne of France would rule the land of Scotland equally beside the young Mary when it came their time to reign.

They were in effect signing over all power and authority in Scotland to Roman Catholic France.

The officials, whose job it was to sign the papers and get the marriage contract in place, arrived in Dieppe with great pomp and ceremony *en route* to negotiate with the King of France, Henry II.

How disappointed Knox must have been when he realised that two of the officials acting for Mary de Guise and her court were James Stewart and Erskine of Dun, whose names had been on the letter asking him to return to Scotland.

'It's all been for nothing,' he said between gritted teeth. Another letter was on his desk, this time from Geneva. The congregation there had generously let him go, now they were generously asking him to return. 'I won't let my pride stop me from doing the Lord's work,' John said to himself. So he returned – full of regrets, but glad to be returning to his wife, his young son, Nathanael, and to Geneva.

Realising that the situation in Scotland was getting worse rather than better, he started to sign his name differently when writing letters – a secret name that only true friends would recognise, 'John Sinclair'. Sinclair had been his mother's maiden name.

In his letters, he openly shared his brokenness and disappointment, 'Sometimes I feel a sob and a groan as I long to hear Christ Jesus openly preached in my native country – even if it means my death.'

The whole situation with Mary of Stewart persuaded John to publish his thoughts on 'The monstrous regiment of Women.' More and more battled and bewildered believers were making their way to Geneva – a refuge of safety and a harbour of peace amongst the storms of persecution. Female rulers tortured, while their heads held crowns and their hands held power. Whatever Knox's views were on women – on these women: Guise, Stewart, Tudor – he was right.

Trouble upon trouble came to stalk John during this time in Geneva. Bad news was never far away. Marjorie was in weak health with another baby on the way. Everyone in that little family was in bad sorts. It was difficult to be refugees and when news that John's two congregations in Berwick and Newcastle had returned to the Roman Catholic Church, it was as if John's heart was split in two.

As they lay in bed one night, the children fast asleep, mother-in-law snoring quietly in the next room, Marjorie clasped John's hand tightly. Was her husband crying, she asked herself. He was. 'Every time I feel the news cannot get any worse, but the next time it always does,' he sighed.

'Help him Lord,' she prayed in the dark.

The prayer was answered.

The next news was entirely different.

'Mary Tudor has died. Elizabeth is queen.'

'God be praised!'

Refugees and the persecuted who had fled from England, cheerfully made their way home. Knox was asked for a third time to return to Scotland and so it was a much more joyful husband that Marjorie was packing for, when the time came for him to make his next journey to Dieppe.

'I will hopefully get a pass to travel through England to see our old congregations in Berwick and Newcastle. I long to see them and to bring them some clear teaching of the Word. You have all you need? Is there anything I should do for you before I leave?'

Marjorie smiled, 'No husband, you have left us well provided for. My mother may complain sometimes and make life a little trying for us both – but you know she holds you and your council in high regard. We arrived here in Geneva penniless refugees, but you leave Geneva now as a burgess of the city. We are well connected and respected. We are in safe hands. The believers here will assist us if we have need.'

John nodded. It was time to go.

However, his plans to travel through England were firmly stamped on. The new Queen Elizabeth, though a Protestant, had, unsurprisingly, taken umbrage at John's 'First Blast against the monstrous regiment of Women.' As a queen of the realm she grasped its power with strong hands – and was not going to let Knox walk at will through her nation.

Queen Elizabeth never really warmed to John Knox after that.

'It seems that my "first blast" has blown every last friend of mine out of England,' John muttered as he made his way back to Scotland by another route.

John Knox is Here!

Knox could not have come at a better time. Mary de Guise was playing her political tricks, trying to buy off the Lords with promises she didn't intend to keep. She had her favourites in power – there wasn't a position of authority in the land that was not filled by a Frenchman. And when the Scottish Lords asked for freedom of worship, all she would say was 'I'd banish every last one of you, even if you all preached as faithfully as St Paul.'

She then arrogantly decided to summon the Protestant preachers to answer charges laid against them. The preachers agreed to this without fear. A great number of their supporters accompanied them. And just before the day of their trial the call went out, 'John Knox is here!'

The news spread like wildfire – there's no other way to describe it. From person to person, from village to town the news was spread by shepherds, fishermen, travellers. Soon the whole land knew that its longed for preacher had returned – home at last. They took heart!

John Knox then headed for Perth, where the other preachers and reformers were gathered, to stand before the Regent to answer her accusations. These men had come in peace, unarmed. She, however refused to recognise this peaceful gathering. John Knox preached a powerful sermon against the lying, devious ways of Mary de Guise and those like her. However, after the congregation had returned home, a Roman Catholic priest turned up at the church and pronounced the Mass. This ignited what was a very volatile situation anyway ... and the people revolted.

What they did distressed Knox greatly. A large crowd of the poor and destitute broke into a monastery to make off with what possessions they could. Knox never condoned violence or destruction of property. 'If they had just contented themselves to destroying the images that would have been fine, but to become common thieves, that does not put our new church in a good light,' he sighed.

James Barron, a man whom Knox had stayed with in the past, nodded his head in agreement, but added some wise words ... 'You're right of course, John, but you can see how badly these people have been treated. It's the month of May, we're just out of winter and the harvests are not in yet. This is a hard time of year for the poor of our land. Now consider that monastery – there were just eight people in it. How much beef, wine, beer and ale came out of those stores – and other provisions too? I'm just thankful that there was no bloodshed.'

'Yes, that is a mercy,' John agreed.

That night John looked out of his window on a land he had thought never to see again. Even now he wondered if Scotland would ever have freedom of worship, but he had to admit something had been lit.

'Has my arrival here been a spark in the hands of God to light this land once more?'

Even as he climbed into his bed that night, across Scotland men were rediscovering lost courage and faith. French officers received letters warning them to return to their own shores. Small congregations gained backbone and conviction. Perhaps the most audacious action was the note left pinned to Mary de Guise's pillow, while she was attending the Mass.

'To fight against the Kirk is to fight against God.'

But Mary de Guise wasn't called a she-wolf for nothing. It would take more than a note on a pillow to scare her. Agreements and treaties were made between the Regent and the people of the Reformed faith, gathered in Perth. But again, John Knox had doubts. He had never trusted in princes ... he wasn't going to start trusting in Regents either.

He was right to be canny. Mary de Guise threw all the treaties out the window and marched into Perth with her troops.

However, the ordinary people were behind the Reformation, great men and noble joined the ranks too and rallied at St Andrews once again.

At first it had seemed that not all was going to go the reformers' way. The Bishop of St Andrews hurled abuse at Knox and would not let him preach in his chapel. The Lord's Day soon approached and the military men and nobles, who had accompanied John, simply did not know what was the best course of action.

'Mary de Guise has made good headway and is about twelve miles away. Should we advance on St Andrews or hold off until a more opportune time? There are plenty of spears and weapons in the city and people enough to use them against us.'

'Aye,' another chipped in. 'But they may yet come over to our side. Who knows, but it might just be the bluster of the bishop we're hearing.'

'We haven't heard anything that could back that up,' was the next argument.

John overheard their discussion and quietly, but firmly interrupted them.

> I can't with good conscience delay the preaching of Christ. St Andrews was the first place where God called me to the dignity of preaching. I was torn away from it by the tyranny of France and the plots of bishops, as you well know. While I was suffering in the galleys, wrenched from my homeland, it was my assured hope that one day I would preach in St Andrews once more before I departed this life. So, my Lords, it is to the astonishment of many that you see me here today – I am back in the same place where I was first called to the office of a preacher. I beseech you therefore do not stop me – I do not come here with a weapon or any man defending me. I just crave to preach.

So on the 11th of June, John Knox stood below the steeple of St Andrews Cathedral – and preached.

His sermon convicted his congregation so much that afterwards many rose up and removed forever the gilded Madonnas and idolatrous statues; making a bonfire of them so that all that was left was a pile of charcoal and ash.

Someone muttered as the congregation left the smoking pile, 'The bishop's not going to like this,' and that was true. The bishop took to his heels and in a flurry of cape and mitre, fled to the refuge of Mary de Guise.

She was just as incensed about the situation and once again went into battle mode. There was a small village not that far from St Andrews which, if captured, would be of crucial importance to her battle plans. However, before Mary de Guise and her troops could make it to the village, news of her plans had reached St Andrews. The Lords, who were by then entrenched in the city, immediately took a hundred horsemen and a few foot soldiers and secured the village for themselves.

Mary was unfazed. She just decided to fight on. It did not look good for the Reformation troops. She outnumbered them considerably – but just when it appeared that all was lost, support arrived from Lothian, the lairds of Ormiston, Calder, Halton, Restalrig and Colston. Lord Ruthven came from Perth with horsemen. The Earl of Rothes also arrived with a considerable force.

On the 13th of June, at Cupar Muir, two Scottish armies faced each other. A thick mist covered the land, hiding the true strength of the Reformation forces. Mary de Guise, full of confidence, commanded the troops to advance, but when the mist lifted an entirely different situation presented itself.

'What did you say?' Mary de Guise screamed at the top of her voice.

'We have counted body after body of troops, Your Majesty, far more than we have planned for. There are at least 1000 spears as well as guns and cavalry.'

'How many cavalry?' she growled.

'It's hard to say,' the officer trembled. 'We believe they have arranged them in such a way that it makes it impossible to estimate their true number .... But there are more than we reckoned ....'

Throwing her riding gloves on the ground in a fit of temper, Mary de Guise hissed between gritted teeth, 'Make a truce then and be quick about it.'

A truce was signed and great rejoicing resulted.

Mary de Guise, of course, just waited her time. She had no intention of ever keeping a word made to any rebel.

Trust Not in Princes

Some weeks later – the rejoicing made after the truce turned flat. 'You're always telling us, Knox, that we should not put our trust in princes ... it seems that we never learn,' Henry Balnaves was back with Knox in St Andrews and was reminiscing with his old friend once more. St Andrews held some fond memories for them ... and some less so.

'Mary de Guise cannot be trusted with anything,' Knox explained, 'but the people always fall for her tricks,' he sighed. 'What have you heard of Lord Douglas and Cockburn recently,' Knox asked. 'The last time we met Cockburn was in England and our paths crossed when the young King Edward was on the throne.'

'Yes,' Henry Balnaves nodded. 'Cockburn has crossed and recrossed the border often. He swore allegiance to King Edward. Scotland then declared him a traitor in 1548. When Queen Mary took power after her brother's death, her Catholicism didn't appeal to Cockburn so he tried to come back to Scotland, but was arrested. I'm not sure why he tried to come back instead of going abroad. It wasn't as though there was anything left for him here.'

'I had heard Ormiston House was demolished by the Scottish crown. But what of Alexander –

what have you heard of him, or the two Douglas boys.'

Henry scratched his head as he tried to remember, 'Alexander is abroad and that's about all I know of him at the moment, he travels a lot. The Douglas boys are growing fast – Francis will soon be making a name for himself in one way or another. He's intelligent and I've heard from his father that he has the makings of an honourable man. The younger one is catching up on him, but still seems to prefer adventure to books.'

John smiled, so much time had passed since those days of Latin texts and grammar books, and now he was on the brink of a new life, where he could almost taste freedom and danger in each breath.

Henry Balnaves looked out to sea and said, 'Well, now that this fruitless truce is over with, we've decided that our Christian brethren in Perth should be relieved from their French occupiers. Who knows, John, perhaps we'll be hearing you preach in Perth next?'

On Saturday the 25th of June, this was exactly what took place. All the church buildings in Perth were cleared of the altars that Mary de Guise had set up.

'Another bloodless victory,' Henry slapped John Knox on the back as he left the chapel that day.

John nodded, 'Thanks be to God. I have no desire to shed blood – just to preach God's Word and give him glory. Though when we made our way through Scone, I have to admit I was afraid that it would turn into a blood-bath. When the bishop's son took out his sword and ran through that poor man ....'

'Poor man,' Henry shook his head. 'He was looting – and that leads to indiscipline ... but I'm loathe to tell the people to leave behind these treasures when the church has been stealing from their families for years. But now we have St Andrews, Perth and Stirling. Mary de Guise must be shaking in her slippers – the way is wide open for us to take Edinburgh. Can you smell victory, John, can you?'

Henry Balnaves punched the air in excitement, mounted his horse and went to join some of the other lairds, who were eagerly pouring over battle plans and maps.

'It has only been eight weeks since I landed at Leith,' John whispered. 'Have we taken a whole country without losing one life?'

When they marched into the capital city, their enemies fled before them, and on the 1st of July, John Knox preached at St Giles Cathedral in Edinburgh.

But it was a short-lived dream of two months. Mary de Guise returned in force and took back Edinburgh once again. For those who would be put to the stake as soon as Mary got her claws in them, the only thing they could do was flee – John Knox was one of that number. But he left with one comfort in his heart, they would not give up St Giles.

'Our dear brother, John Willock, has consented to stay in order to offer comfort to the believers as they continue the church there. He does this at risk of his own life.'

The news that filtered out of Edinburgh to the vanquished reformers gave them some small cheer.

Even though the crown had tried to take the Kirk from them, reformers still worshipped in St Giles cathedral. The enemy had to watch as they continued to pray and preach and take communion in full view of everyone.

John Knox, however, had one regret – throughout those eight glorious weeks his wife, Marjorie, had not been with him, so he sent a letter to Queen Elizabeth via her trusted servant, Cecil – a simple plea to give his wife, children and mother-in-law safe passage through England, so that they could be reunited once more.

John also had to appeal to Queen Elizabeth for money. Elizabeth, though only a 'weak and feeble woman' had changed the financial prosperity of her country for the better. England's coffers were pretty full and Scotland's were running on empty. The reformers had even less money, so Knox took pen to paper once more to appeal to England for cash to pay for soldiers, footmen, and horsemen. John appealed to England's fear of France. It would not do for the Reformation troops to go hungry and unpaid for. That would allow France, through Mary de Guise, to become masters of Scotland – and France were never friends of England.

But while Knox was warning England of the truth – Mary de Guise was cunningly soothing the lairds and dukes of her realm with sweet little lies of her good intentions. She did not harbour ill will to the reformers, rather their disagreements were but trifles and they could all soon be at peace once more.

If all you did was listen to her words, you would have been taken for a complete fool … the number of French forces that increased in Scotland told the true story.

Elizabeth's money couldn't have come at a better time. When the news arrived, Knox quickly handed the letter over to Henry Balnaves and the other lairds. Balnaves set off at once to a secret destination where the money would be handed over.

The reformers then marched on Edinburgh to again make demands of the Regent. Their demands were that she should send her French soldiers packing, to which Mary de Guise replied in a most offended manner.

'How dare you presume to command me!' the words just about jumped off the page as she wrote them fiercely and with great anger. 'This realm does not need to be conquered by any force as it has been conquered by marriage. The French soldiers are not strangers as you presume, but are naturalized citizens of this land. I am not going to send any man away unless I think it necessary.'

Reading the document amongst themselves later that evening, even the great military commanders shook their heads. What Mary de Guise was saying was true.

'Conquered by marriage, can you believe it?' Knox leaned back in his chair, drumming his long fingers against the arm. 'That woman has planned this from the moment she gave birth, if not before. She has plotted and schemed every last detail. That child was never going to marry Edward VI – she was earmarked for a French monarch from day one. But we do not trust in princes – we trust in the Lord whose plans are far greater than hers and he's been planning since before the beginning of time.'

'So do you think we have the right to depose this woman from her position of power?' one of the lairds asked Knox.

Everyone in the room had read or heard of John's opinion about female rulers. His 'blast' against the 'Monstrous Regiment of Women' was well known … so they did not expect John to say what he said next.

'I don't think we should depose her, but remove her from power for a while, until we can be more certain of her.'

Henry Balnaves almost choked on the bowl of soup he was devouring at the table, 'Until we can be more certain of her? John, is that you I'm hearing and are you talking of Mary de Guise?'

'Yes, Henry, that is my opinion. You all may make up your own minds.'

And they did – Mary de Guise was suspended, much to her extreme annoyance. But it would take more than a declaration by the reformers to push Mary de Guise out. She had spies skulking through the capital and they saw things as they truly were. The reformers were putting up a good fight, but their provisions and troops were not as numerable as it at first appeared.

Henry Balnaves approached Knox one day with some grave news. 'We need more money. There's a possibility of someone in the borders who is willing to give us a sizeable donation.'

'How much?' John asked

'Just over 4,000 crowns,' Henry replied. 'But what I really want to ask you is what you think of the young Alexander Cockburn.'

John smiled, warmly, 'A fine young man ... I'm glad he is back from his travels. He is one that I'm delighted to see in our number. He's brave and has considerable experience. Above all, he's trustworthy and that's a quality you can't have enough of. He would be a good choice to send as a courier.'

Henry nodded, 'That's what I think. I'll give him his instructions and he'll leave tonight under cover of darkness. It's a dangerous journey and he'll have to keep his wits about him, but, as you say, we can trust him.'

However, later, Knox was saddened to hear the news that Alexander had been attacked just as he had left the secret venue. All 4,000 crowns had been stolen from him – everything the Reformed forces had been relying on to buy provisions and pay their troops. Now there was virtually nothing left – and Alexander was badly injured.

Still more disasters came upon them. The French troops, cunning as ever, chose the Lord's Day as the best day to make attack on the city of Edinburgh. They knew that most of the lairds and a good many of the soldiers would be at church, and after the service would go immediately to eat their dinner. They also knew, through intelligence reports, that the cavalry were elsewhere.

The French troops attacked with some skill, but were chased back to Leith. Even though they failed –

they also succeeded because panic spread throughout the city when a false rumour arose that French troops were now in Edinburgh. Later the French intercepted food supplies that were making their way to the Reformed troops. Some of the lairds went on the attack, but then found themselves pinned between the sea and a large body of French troops.

'Thankfully, they were not completely cut off,' Knox muttered as he bathed the wounds of yet another young soldier who had just made it back with his life. 'Thirty men have been lost this day and there are many injured.'

Henry Balnaves hung his head in sorrow, all morale stolen from him. 'Perhaps we should have done what you asked after all, John,' he sighed. 'We could have sent an envoy to England to ask for more help, for Elizabeth's support, but we didn't. I suppose pride got in the way.'

'You were complacent, my friend,' Knox replied. 'We all were. I could have put more force into my words, but my passion is for the pulpit not for politics. Now I'm afraid that we are going to have to flee this city once again.'

Henry sat down heavily in a chair and rested his head in his hands, a picture of grief and disappointment.

Fighting on in Faith

On the 6th of November, the Reformed troops left the city under cover of darkness, but not unnoticed. Many, who because of homes or families couldn't leave the city, followed them with stones and abuse, shouting at them for abandoning them to the French.

Knox and the other reformers felt that once again the dream of a free Scotland was slipping from their grasp.

The following Lord's Day, in Stirling, a discouraged group of believers met together to listen once more to John Knox preach. He took for his text a Psalm – Psalm 80:4.

> *O Lord God of Hosts how long wilt thou be angry against the prayer of thy people?*
>
> *Thou feedest them with the bread of tears, and givest them tears to drink in great measure.*
>
> *Thou makest us a strife unto our neighbours, and our enemies laugh among themselves.*

John encouraged his sorrowful congregation to fight against the temptation to think that God had turned away from them and was not listening to their prayers.

'We must fight on in this battle of faith. But why has God let us experience these troubles?' It was a question that everyone was asking in that congregation.

John continued, 'Before we started this battle, when we had neither earl nor lord to comfort us, we called upon God: we took him for our protector, defence and only refuge. We didn't brag about how many we were, or of our strength or our plots or strategies ... we only cried out to God ... but since this lord and that has joined our company we have heard nothing but, "Lord so and so will bring us so many hundreds of spears; the laird of this land has credit in that country; if that earl joins our number we'll have no one trouble us."'

John preached against the pride that had brought the reformers to put their trust in soldiers and nobility and the forces and coin they could bring. 'Turn us again, O Lord God of Hosts,' John cried out. 'Cause thy face to shine, and we shall be saved.'

It was a sermon that challenged and encouraged the sorry bunch of believers. One wrote in a letter afterwards that 'Knox's words were a better rallying cry than 500 trumpets in a battle.'

Now that that sermon was over, John simply felt the need to return to St Andrews for there, in a little house in the middle of the city, his wife and children waited eagerly to hold him, and his mother-in-law was in great need of some gospel preaching!

John's work of letter writing increased with a pace, sometimes it was so hard he could barely finish with a legible signature. Marjorie noticed her husband's trouble when he returned to St Andrews and did her best to write as many of his letters as she could, sometimes taking down his dictation late into the night. John still used his assumed name, John

Sinclair, so that if they were read by eyes who were not supposed to read them, they would not recognise the letters as coming from John Knox. Knox was sending pleas to England for help, reports to Calvin in Geneva about the progress of the Reformation in Scotland and requests for much needed books. He even started to think about writing a book himself on the Reformation in Scotland that was happening under his feet.

The Reformation troops and their lairds still had great battles to fight, and in the winter months too. Some of the men fought solidly, in their clothes, for twenty-one days, not one of them taking off his boots.

Knox and his family sheltered in St Andrews where John preached to disconsolate crowds, cheering them on through the gospel. He reminded them of Peter and the disciples in the boat. They all knew the end of that story. The disciples would be safe, Peter would not drown. Perhaps they felt that they did not know the end of their own story as yet, but it was the same God who was on their side.

'God grant that ye may acknowledge his hand, after you see how he has delivered you,' John exclaimed.

But Mary de Guise also fought on, she had a daughter who she believed would one day be the Queen of Scotland and of France. The Regent was laying down plots thick and fast … and in the midst of her triumph she foolishly exclaimed, 'Where is John Knox now, where is his God? My God is stronger than his!'

Someone with little faith might have felt she was right, as one morning the French made swift progress towards St Andrews. In the distance, sails could be seen crossing the North Sea. It brought back horrible memories to the St Andrews' residents.

However, on closer inspection one voice called out, 'That's not French ships, that's English ships.'

It appeared that of all those late night letters that John and Marjorie had written, some had arrived safely, to the right people, at the right time … God's time!

It was said that the French fled in defeat twice as fast as they had advanced in victory.

There was great rejoicing when the news came through that the French fleet had been wrecked on the Dutch coast. As John and Marjorie looked on at the celebrations, Marjorie turned to her husband and asked, 'Is that it then?'

'What's it, my dear?'

'Is that the end to all your politics and intrigue? Will there be any more secret letters or coded messages?'

John scratched his head. 'That would be nice,' he thought. 'Maybe it could work.' He had, for some time, realised that politics was not where his passion lay. He knew he wasn't called by God to that vocation.

'If God wills it, my love, but with this country, who can tell. Many in this congregation of ours say I am too extreme. I think that is a good enough reason to extract myself from politics. My study calls to me and I have many books to search out and read.'

And as Mary de Guise began her final journey from this life to the next, still scheming, still fighting till her last breath, refusing prayers and sending codes, John Knox preached once more in St Giles.

> *They that wait upon the Lord shall renew their strength; they shall lift up their wings as the eagles; they shall run and not be weary; they shall walk, and not faint.*

Knox needed the strength of the Lord in the days and years to come. Forming a national church was not easy. It needed someone who could tackle difficulties with strength and face problems with endurance. It was no ordinary task, making a church for the people, of the people, governed by the people – and all for the glory of God.

The idolatry of Rome was to be thrown out and the whole nation was asked to trust in the Lord God.

Princes of the realm had been futile, popes and priests of the church had failed miserably ... God's Word was true. The people were to trust not in princes, but trust in the Lord. Knox formed a plain statement of faith for this new kirk or church. A Confession of Faith and a large Book of Discipline were produced in a very short space of time.

Knox was not only moulding a church, he was forming a nation, a nation that would influence the world through its faith, politics and ingenuity.

Knox's heart for freedom, and in particular the freedom of the gospel, was at the heart of everything he did and wrote.

Though this new church and its new publications were made by Knox – he didn't want to make a collection of additional strict rules for worship over and above what was given in Scripture. He wanted people to worship with freedom, worshipping from the Word of God, using passages of Scripture that appealed to them personally. Knox didn't want to put clamps or chains on the Scottish believers – so he didn't.

One afternoon, during those heady days when the Kirk was in its first flush of youth, John and Marjorie went for a walk along the cliff – leaving Marjorie's mother with the children. It was a break from household duties for Marjorie, but for Knox it was some cherished time with his wife. She was eager to ask him questions about the new church and what his hopes were for it.

'The Lord's Table has always been an important part of your ministry, John,' Marjorie acknowledged. 'It gave me such comfort to remember the Lord's death last Lord's Day. When I remember how in the Roman Catholic Church we focussed so much on this or that way of doing things, on the garments and vestments, on the ceremony and ritual. Now I relish the simplicity.'

John nodded, 'The Lord's Table, as we administer it, is even different to the Church of England. There is no division – it is the Lord's Table and not a Table of any one church. So we open the Lord's Table to any believer. We differ in baptism too. Children are so important. I don't just want parents attending a child's baptism – the whole church should be there too; the whole family of God. I also don't hold with this papish idea that children, who die unbaptised, go straight to hell. That's not in the Scripture. It's just another deception conjured up by years of heretical priests, obsessed with fleecing an uneducated population, in order to fill their own pockets.'

'Lord Balnaves remembers your catechism exercises in St Andrews, when you had the Douglas boys and Alexander to teach,' Mary added.

John nodded, 'Yes, I still hold to that idea. When you teach the children, the adults learn too. I've written a great deal about teaching children in the Book of Discipline.'

'Yes, I've read some of that. I particularly like how you instruct ministers to visit the more remote areas, so that children from far off villages and communities don't get forgotten. They need teaching too.'

'You're right, Marjorie, they do. For in our new Kirk no one is to be admitted to the Lord's Table who does not have a knowledge of God's law and the commandments; prayer; sacraments and the true knowledge of the Lord Jesus Christ.'

'There's just one problem,' Marjorie quizzed. 'How many of these children can read? Their parents can't read, none of those outlying villages will have schools.'

'I see you haven't read that section of my book entitled, 'The Necessity of Schools'. God hasn't decided that humanity is to be taught by angels … we are to be taught by men. Men are all born ignorant of God and we don't have miraculous revelations anymore – so the only way to teach people about God is to teach them. I want every church to appoint a schoolmaster.'

Marjory's eyes opened wide in astonishment. 'Is that possible?' she asked, incredulously.

'I believe that with the Lord's help it is possible,' John declared. 'I may not live to see it fully realised, however.'

John continued to share with his wife the plans he had for the formation of this new national church of Scotland. There were to be properly audited accounts so that corruption would not gain a foothold. Ministers were to be accountable to the people in their congregations. Elders were to administer correction if it was needed. The money that had been received from the now deposed Roman Catholic Church was to be divided into three parts – one to help run the church, one to be given to the poor and another to be devoted to the setting up of schools.

As the couple turned for home once more, John asked his wife if she was ready for their return journey to Edinburgh.

'Yes, the packing is done, the bills are paid. Are you ready for St Giles?'

John just smiled … St Andrews may have been where he had first preached, but Edinburgh he felt was in great need now of the Word of God and he was more than ready to give it.

Mary Queen of Scots

The preaching in St Giles wasn't that easy. There were people there who struggled daily with doubts about God and their own salvation. However, John had had years of experience of this type of troubled pilgrim – his mother-in-law had constantly been seeking peace with God. Her emotions in turmoil and her thoughts confused, she had often turned to John for help. In fact, it seemed as though he alone was the one who could calm her troubled spirit in these matters.

Politics continued to haunt the city as the new Queen Mary still refused to support the treaty of Leith that her mother had signed. Mary de Guise had ignored it, her daughter seemed to be cut from the same cloth, albeit a more fashionable French one. The population of Scotland though, did not expect this young queen to make Scotland her power base.

'You'll not get a fancy piece like her coming across the water. She's destined for greater things, is Mary Stewart!'

'Aye. She's going to be Queen of France no less!'

'Huh … and she'll not want to dirty her pretty little French shoes in Scotland – even if it is the land of her birth.'

'I've heard that although she's a bonny young lass, she's got her mother's steely nature.'

The gossipers were right. Reports had come back from France that Mary had been present at the hanging, one spring day, of fifty-seven French Protestants.

However, what Mary did in France stayed in France and her people didn't pay much heed to a woman who would more than likely stay there. Christmas drew near and snow lay frosted on the ground – the smell of meats roasting and preserved fruits wafted up from kitchens. One house, however, was not celebrating.

Knox and many reformers did not believe in celebrating Christmas Day – but this year Knox was spending as much time as he could at Marjorie's bedside. As the last month of the year drew to a close, it was obvious Mrs Knox wouldn't see another New Year. The wife and mother would leave her husband and two young sons to the care of God before she died at only twenty-seven years of age.

Knox continued to preach and perform his duties, but friends whispered behind hands and in private that he was a changed man.

'He's never made friends easily, but with this attitude he's not going to keep the friends he has,' was one man's comment as John Knox walked gravely away from the Sunday service.

'Marjorie isn't cold in her grave yet,' his wife exclaimed, poking her husband in the ribs as she said it. 'Let him be.'

'He has burdens to bear and two young lads to bring up on his own,' another old woman interrupted.

Anyone else who wanted to comment on the 'surly' nature of the preacher was soon silenced.

Knox was not the only one to lose a spouse that year. The young Scottish queen, who had had such high hopes of ruling the nation of France and Scotland, suddenly became a widow. Mary de Guise had plotted long and hard for her daughter to become ruler of one of the greatest nations in Europe – and it had all come to nothing.

The Scottish Lords thought it was time to send a delegation to France in order to find out what this young queen was really like. Now, it was quite likely that Scotland would end up with a young, widowed, queen on their hands. France didn't want her. She had no position there now. They had princesses enough of their own. Scotland could have her back.

However, the country Mary was returning to was different now. St Giles wasn't filled to the gunnels with icons and gilded Madonnas. Mary had left, as a young child, a country that had been under the control of the Roman Catholic Church. She herself was a staunch Roman Catholic and insisted on celebrating the Mass regularly. Scotland was now a Protestant country. It wasn't bowing and scraping to princes or priests. For this red-headed, passionate, eighteen-year-old, life was going to hold a surprise or two.

As John sat in his study preparing for his next sermon, at which he would serve the Lord's Table, he heard again the loud boom of cannon. This time it wasn't an invading army, but a salute to a returning monarch. Mary de Guise's child had come home. By all reports she had a 'bonny face'. But Knox knew that a fresh young face could hide a bitter soul.

Some feared she would come with an army behind her, but in fact she landed on Scottish soil accompanied by no more than a selection of poets and musicians and some rather dashing young gentlemen. She didn't really need anything else. Her winsome ways and cunning femininity won her battles for her. Where her mother had failed with her plots and battles – Mary succeeded with her lips and eyelashes – and a cunning head on her shoulders.

Knox was disappointed at how easily she persuaded the lairds to allow her to celebrate the Mass – which had so recently been made illegal. He looked on, astonished at how this young girl made fools of men twice her age.

Mary's popularity grew with her people – both the ordinary man and the noble lord felt drawn to her side. However, this was often at Knox's expense. Everyone flocked to the lovely young queen, her parties and jollity attracted the rich and influential to court, few could resist her … but Knox.

From the pulpit he made it clear that he did not condone the fact that, after such a short space of time, the new church was doing its utmost to accommodate the young woman. 'If she'd arrived here with ten thousand armies it would not have scared me half as much as this girl who has arrived with that one Mass!'

His absence from court was conspicuous to say the least and Mary didn't like it. To have the most famous man in Scotland preaching against her was bad enough, but for him to blatantly avoid her company was unthinkable.

Men usually gravitated towards her presence as moths to a flame. Surely Knox was no different. She decided to summon the grumpy old Scot to her courtroom. Then her charms were sure to succeed.

However, Knox had hardly been in the room five minutes when they were arguing. Mary accused him of rebelling against her mother and herself. 'You've even written a book against me,' she complained. 'You've caused trouble and slaughter in England, and have been a traitor against this land. I'm certain you're involved in witchcraft. You couldn't have accomplished what you have without it!' She flounced her skirts and glared at him with piercing eyes.

Knox cleared his throat before making his reply. 'If by rebellion you mean teaching the people the Word of God in sincerity, to rebuke idolatry, and to encourage them to worship God according to his Word – then, yes, I am guilty. I have, I admit, published the book that you mention. But if you can get someone to prove to me that I was wrong in what I wrote, I will willingly confess my error and ignorance.

'However, the book was mostly written against that evil queen of England, Mary Tudor. And as to your accusation of witchcraft you only have to read my sermons to find out that I have regularly preached against the practice.'

'Well, that may be,' she replied haughtily, 'but you have taught the people to receive another religion, one that the crown has not allowed. How can that be a doctrine of God, when God commands people to obey their rulers?'

Knox was ready with his counter-argument, 'Madame, right religion did not originate from worldly princes, but from the eternal God alone. Your subjects are not bound to form their religion by your desires or wishes. If all of Abraham's descendants had joined the religion of Pharaoh, or if all the apostles had followed the religion of Nero – what faith would we have now?'

'None of these men rebelled with the sword,' Mary added, quite proud that she was holding her own.

'But, Madame, they certainly did resist, though not by the sword, because God had not given them that means or opportunity.'

'So you think that subjects, if they have the power, then have the right to resist?'

'Yes,' John concluded, 'if our rulers go beyond their boundaries they must be resisted. What if a father goes mad and tries to harm his children? Should he not be seized and have his weapons taken from him? So it should be with rulers that would murder the children of God that are subject to them. To cast them into prison until they be of a more sober mind is not an act of disobedience, but obedience as it agrees with the will of God.'

Mary was astonished at what she had just heard. She was no longer in Paris – that was for certain. With a toss of her auburn curls, she turned towards Knox where her steely gaze met his resolute one. Other courtiers looked on in hushed silence.

'I perceive that my subjects shall obey you and not me. They will do what they want and not what I command. I am to be subject to them and not them to me.'

'I pray that that will not be true,' John replied. 'Both princes and subjects must obey God. God commands a king to be as a foster father to his church and that a queen nourish his people.'

'But I will never nourish your church,' she spat out. 'I nourish the true church, the Church of Rome.'

'But that is not the true church, for five hundred years or more it has been in decline from that purity of religion that the apostles taught.'

'My conscience says this is not so,' Mary shot back.

'But conscience, Madame, needs knowledge and I am afraid that you have none.'

Mary could not believe that such a man as this Knox could dare to address her in such a manner. 'No knowledge?' she exclaimed. 'Why, I have both heard and read.'

'So did the Jews who crucified our Lord,' Knox retorted. 'You have only heard priests and cardinals preach.'

'Well, they interpret Scripture one way and you another – who am I to believe?' she asked, snappishly.

John pointed the young queen to the Word of God.

And then it being late afternoon the queen was called to the dining chamber. John had one further opportunity to speak to her before she left. He wished her well and prayed that God would bless her in this new land of hers.

As she quitted the courtroom, the young queen's furrowed brow betrayed a concern that she had finally met someone, a man no less, whom she could not move or alter.

John left Holyrood Palace convinced that the young monarch of Scotland had a 'proud mind, a crafty wit and a stubborn heart against God and his truth.'

However, Mary didn't need or seek after Knox's approval, she had plenty of people willing to obey her every wish and command. Some even tried to second guess how they could please their queen. One suggestion was that the new Kirk should not be allowed to have public meetings without her permission. Mary really warmed to that idea. Knox thundered against it. 'If you take away our freedom of assembly you take away the very gospel from us.'

Nobody stood up against the queen's extravagance at Holyrood. She spent money hand over fist – taking what rightfully belonged to the new Kirk and using it to buy furnishings and fashions. Money that would have been spent on the poor and on education was whittled away on trifles.

Some of the Protestant Lords sincerely hoped that Mary would become Protestant ... but Knox knew that Mary was a de Guise. He had seen de Guise power in action. Not that it bothered him that much. He had squared up to many powerful people before, but he had not been afraid of any – the young gentlewoman, though queen of the realm, held no fear for him.

He distrusted her, criticized her, pitied her even – but was not afraid. She mourned her husband with a Requiem Mass one day and then danced to dawn the next. She flirted with a young courtier and then sent a besotted lover to the scaffold. She could send a man to death with one hand and then charm a nation with a smile.

In fact, her smiles gained Mary much popularity John noted one day. He had been summoned to visit her in the castle of Lochleven. The queen wished to discuss what should be done about some priests who had broken the law by celebrating the Mass in public. Although it wasn't a very serious punishment that they received – it was surprising enough that they were punished at all. Even Knox had been somewhat taken in by the young woman's behaviour.

But Knox still had his doubts, something was niggling at him. 'I wonder if she punished those priests simply in order to appease the Protestants? Mary is showing great tolerance,' he muttered under his breath. Henry Balnaves was puffing his pipe in the corner of John's study that overlooked the bustling royal mile outside.

'I wouldn't be so eager to criticise her if I were you,' Henry declared. 'If you'd seen her, John, the other day as she addressed parliament,' Henry smiled.

John huffed as Henry Balnaves went on to describe the beautiful young queen as she progressed down the Royal Mile on a pure white horse. 'She was every inch the monarch. The speech she made, John, was everything you would desire from a queen ... and she wrote every word herself.'

'I wouldn't put it past her,' John muttered.

Henry glared at his friend. 'Your friends are right – you're becoming a sullen old man.'

John returned the glare. 'Sullen old man – I've every right to be a sullen old man. Time makes me old and this land and its gentry are making me sullen. We forget that this young woman is still a de Guise – so there's a plot somewhere. She's going to be the people's new favourite, whatever happens,' John reasoned.

'Well,' said Henry, his very tone a warning, 'be careful that you don't become their old favourite. And don't worry about Her Majesty … if you had heard her speak and seen her smiles ….' Henry went on and on about the new young queen, while John switched off and stared blankly out the window.

'I don't care what they say,' John thought to himself. 'She is plotting … something is afoot.'

Treason and Scandal

John Knox was right. Mary was tired of being a widow, she wanted a match, someone with power and strength and a Roman Catholic ... a bit of romance would be nice too.

There was a suitor that suited her, King Philip of Spain's son. Key individuals around both thrones surmised that Mary's marriage to a prince of Spain might be a good way of getting the Pope back in power in Scotland.

Then the plans for Mary's marriage to the heir of the Spanish throne became public, but no one was willing to speak out against it. The lairds who had once appeared to be such staunch supporters of the Reformation became weak and simpering under the power of the queen. All that John could do was preach! So preach he did. And he made a point of speaking directly to the Protestant lairds.

'I have been with you in the most extreme dangers. I shall never forget that day when you, my lords, with shame and fear, left this town. Shall this be your thankfulness to God that you betray his cause, when you have it in your own hands to establish it as you please?

You say, "But the queen will not agree with us". Go and ask her – and if she will not agree with you in God

– you should not agree with her in the devil. May she not steal from you your former strength in the Lord. Then he shall prosper you. But what do I see here? All that I see is a recoiling from Christ Jesus.

'As for the queen's marriage – mark this that whenever the nobility of Scotland, professing the Lord Jesus, consents that an infidel shall be head over your sovereign, you are doing as much as you can to banish Christ Jesus from this realm. You bring God's vengeance on this country; a plague on yourself and small comfort on your queen.'

With this sermon, John succeeded in offending almost everybody.

The Roman Catholics hated him. The Protestant Lords despised him. Mary Queen of Scots did both – and summoned him immediately to her presence. Her ivory cheeks had a distinct fiery glow about them as John approached her throne. Before he could barely take a breath, he was faced with a veritable royal tirade.

'There has never been a queen handled in this way! I have put up with your rough speaking and have sought to please you in any way I can. I have let you approach this throne whenever you pleased, in order to admonish me: and yet I cannot get rid of you!'

At this point the young queen promptly burst into copious tears. 'I vow to God that I shall be revenged!' she sobbed.

John stood silently as a young page boy rushed hither and thither trying to find anything that would do to mop up the young queen's tears. She wept and wailed as the court looked on and John stood quietly until the worst of the storm had passed. Eventually, he managed to get a word in edgeways.

'Your Grace,' he bowed solemnly, 'it is true that I am involved in many controversies, but in regard to my preaching I am not my own master. I must obey the one who commands me to speak plainly and not to flatter people.'

'But what have you to do with my marriage!' Mary yelled.

John shook his head, this was too much to take from a young girl like this – but he mustn't forget that she was the monarch of the realm. 'Your Majesty, let me speak the truth in simple words. My God has not sent me to wait on the courts of princesses or visit the rooms and chambers of ladies – but I have been sent to preach the gospel of Jesus Christ ....' At this point John saw his chance and jumped straight into a gospel message.

'The good news of Jesus Christ has two parts,' he explained. 'Repentance and faith. Now, Madame, in preaching repentance ....'

Mary would hear nothing of repentance. She stood up abruptly from her throne in an attempt to intimidate the bearded old man in front of her. Again she yelled at him, 'What have you to do with my marriage? What have you to do with this country of mine?'

Her words dripped scorn, but John's words spoke of liberty – one that was God-given.

'I am a subject born within that same country,' he retorted. 'God has placed me here and it is my duty to forewarn of things that may be to its hurt ... and this marriage is not to the benefit of this land of mine.'

Mary's tears continued, her courtiers tried to soothe her with flattery while Knox was beginning to tire of the whole scene. Mary flung threats and accusations at him with abandon. 'You are secretly pleased to see me weep,' she reproached him. 'You have no care for your sovereign!'

John attempted to repress a frustrated sigh. 'Madame, I have never delighted in the weeping of any of God's creatures. I can scarcely abide the tears of my own two boys when I have to correct them. Much less can I delight in Your Majesty's tears. But I have not given you any just occasion to be offended. I have but spoken the truth. I will suffer Your Majesty's weeping rather than hurt my conscience or betray my country through my silence.'

Mary's next words were to demand that John Knox leave her presence. 'You can wait there for further orders,' she declared.

So he did. When he stood in the outer chamber it was clear that the courtiers had overheard the whole tirade. No one would speak to him. Men wouldn't look at him. Women did their best to avoid his gaze. Those closest to him would suddenly find something terribly interesting to look at on the tapestry. They stood there in all their glittering glory – while Knox was shunned – an outcast.

John just shrugged his shoulders, for all their snobbery and fine ways this was just another congregation.

'O fair ladies,' he called out to the throng of people awaiting Her Majesty's pleasure. 'How pleasing this life of yours would be if you were to live and then pass straight to heaven with all your fair fashions – but beware of death. It will come whether you wish it or not. Your body will be corrupted, your flesh will decay, be it ever so fair and tender; and I fear that your silly little souls will be so feeble – for they cannot carry with them gold, pearls or precious stones ....'

A messenger from the courtroom approached him with his further instructions. He could go.

John exited the chamber – to the relieved sighs of some and the nervous chuckles of others.

There were some silly souls in the palace that day.

In a few weeks time, though, the shifting of politics meant that it was not the fancy ladies and their gentlemen that appeared silly – John Knox was made out to be a fool by the most foolish people of the court.

'To think that Knox had the audacity to speak against the queen's marriage,' exclaimed a grand-looking dame, dripping in pearls. 'He marched into her very presence to give her a piece of his deluded mind. But the queen had no such plans. It was just a bit of silliness on the part of that mad old preacher. More fool him and his arrogant ways – telling the queen not to marry – when she had no such plans anyway.'

Those were the tales spreading around the capital city. The reality was that the queen had indeed planned to marry the Spanish prince, but the negotiations had gone wrong. The queen's council made up a lie that the story of her marriage was a fiction made up by Knox. Once again the man of God was belittled and laughed at by the court.

As he remained in his study one morning, he heard the last of the queen's advance party, quitting the capital for Her Majesty's trip to the west of the country. Outside, on the Royal Mile, his two sons were returning from a quick excursion in order to see the royal retinue in all its finery.

John asked them if they had seen anything interesting.

'We didn't see the queen. She leaves later on in the week. The advance party have to go ahead in order to prepare the royal camp. They did have a lot of wagons though. One of them was full of some really strange things,' Knox's youngest lad exclaimed.

'And what things were they?' John asked.

'A golden box, a strange-looking statue of a lady, pictures of people I've never seen before – someone said they were saints ... and then there were some relics I think .... What are relics, Father?'

John sighed. He tried to explain to his young son about the evils of the things he had seen in that wagon ... that the Queen of Scotland in effect worshipped idols ... and that it had been a most precious prayer of his to have those idols banished from the land. John taught his young sons about the danger and the sin of worshipping anything or anyone other than the one true God. 'Even if it was the bone of a disciple or some wood from the cross of Christ himself on that wagon, these are not to be worshipped ... for the

Word says, "You shall have no other gods before me and you shall not make for yourself a carved image ... you shall not bow down to them or serve them."

'Beware, my boys, of the teachings of these priests and cardinals ... they would have you believe that you can buy your salvation when it has been bought already through the blood of our Lord and Saviour Jesus Christ. Nothing can change that for it is the truth. You, as a sinner, deserve God's judgement. There is no one, except God's Son, who can take your place before the Almighty. Christ is your only representative. You have no need of icons or relics, saints or priests to stand before God on your behalf. Christ does that for you. You are covered in his righteousness. Remember that, my boys, for I fear that this country has forgotten it already.'

Knox slowly eased himself back into his study chair. When had he become so old, with a sore back and stiff legs? His two young boys scampered up the stairs so easily while now he was struggling to get into bed without pain and discomfort. But the pain in his body wasn't so bad as the pain in his heart.

Knox was now witnessing his worst fear. Some in positions of power in Scotland were supporters of the idolatrous Mass. John heard of the courtiers in the palace who gave their ultimate allegiance to the queen instead the King of Kings; they worshipped the bread that was served at the Mass instead of Jesus Christ the Bread of Life. Mary had been allowed her Mass at Holyrood ... and John could see that it was that small submission that would possibly bring the people of Scotland back into the clutches of a faithless church.

However, there were troublemakers in Knox's camp too. The following week, after all the queen's carriages had left the palace, Knox took his place, as usual, in the pulpit of St Giles. There were some well-known faces missing from the crowd, but John paid no heed. He preached as he always did, with passion and truth.

After the service was over, as John greeted some members of the congregation, he spotted one of the missing faces, with a huge black eye and what looked like a missing tooth. A couple of women were ushering the man out of the church.

'There's been a riot,' someone whispered to John. 'A few of the men from the church went to the Palace of Holyrood to see if any of our congregation were attending the Mass instead of listening to your sermon. Things got out of hand and before anything could be done, both sides were fighting each other, drawing blood even.'

John understood their frustration, but was against all unnecessary bloodshed. He may once have been a bodyguard, but he wasn't a thug, he valued human life. So when John heard this news from the palace, he turned towards the tattle-tale and declared, 'You know that I am most certainly against the Church of Rome – but riots, in the palace? What were you thinking of? You men would have been better attending the preaching of God's Word than raising your fists in the royal court. I'm afraid we haven't heard the end of this.'

And John was right. When Mary returned, she heard the full story and was furious. She threatened Knox and the other reformers with her vengeance.

Knox's congregation persuaded him to write a letter in order to inform other Protestants about what was taking place in Edinburgh. 'Justice must be done,' they exclaimed. 'If Queen Mary has her way, we'll all be in prison or worse.' So Knox did as they asked. However, one of his letters found its way into the hands of a traitor who handed the letter to the queen.

'At last!' Mary thought. 'I have him.' She had the perfect excuse to get John Knox out of her hair for good. He'd had nothing to do with the riots – but that didn't stop her blaming him for them … and the letter was the final proof she needed to put an end to that infuriating preacher for good … or so she thought.

Mary decided to accuse Knox of treason. In the 1500s there were several crimes that were punishable by death … one of which was inciting hatred or harm against your sovereign. This was called treason. If you were caught up in a plot to overthrow the monarch, even if you were overheard to talk of their future death – you would be arrested and then beheaded or burnt at the stake or hung by the neck until dead.

So for John to be accused by his queen of treason was a serious situation indeed. When a knock was heard on the door and Master Maxwell stood there, John realised that this old friend of his wasn't here on a social call.

'He used to be loyal to the true church,' Knox thought as the richly-dressed supporter of the monarch was shown into Knox's study. 'But I've heard he's a supporter of the palace now.'

Maxwell's fine clothes and expensive boots looked out of place amongst John's piles of papers, books and quills. A thin veneer of dust covered the room – the noble guest held a handkerchief to his nose. He may have fought bravely on the side of the Reformation in the past, but now he was playing court to the queen and was more refined in his tastes. Knox ignored the man's snobbish ways and pointed his guest to an empty seat.

Maxwell flicked his handkerchief on the covering before placing himself gingerly on the cushions. Then he launched straight into what he wanted to say, no small talk or pleasantries … that suited Knox fine.

'We know each other well, John, so I feel it's my duty to warn you that you have severely displeased Her Majesty and you must apologise.'

'How have I displeased Her Majesty?' John asked. 'I have done nothing that deserves her displeasure.'

'You have gathered together the people without her permission.'

'But I have done that for over two years now and no one has said anything about it?'

'Well, that was then and this is now,' Maxwell replied tritely.

Knox stood up from his chair, holding a copy of the Scriptures in his hand, 'What was lawful to me last year is still lawful because my God is unchangeable.'

Maxwell stood to look John eyeball to eyeball, 'Do as you wish, but you will be sorry for it if you do not submit your will to the queen.'

'I have never been an adversary to the queen,' John said, 'except in the matter of religion. I am sure that you wouldn't want me to bow to Her Majesty in that respect.'

John waited for a reply, hoping to hear something that would indicate Maxwell's continuing support for the Reformed cause.

But instead, the man just shrugged his shoulders and made his way towards the door. He did, however, say one last thing, 'You are wise enough, John, but those who stood with you in the past may not stand with you today.'

Knox replied, 'God is my friend and I depend on his promise and prefer his glory to my life and worldly profit, so I pay little regard to how men behave towards me.'

Maxwell exited onto the street, leaving Knox to stare after him. 'Another name I can add to the list of men who have deserted the cause of Christ.'

Maxwell wouldn't be the last. Other men, whom Knox had once counted on as friends, soon began to criticise him for his treatment of the queen. Any man who wanted to be found in favour with Mary just had to accuse Knox or belittle him to make the monarch smile.

But there was one well-connected man who had John's best interests at heart, the queen's advocate, Spens of Condie. He had been brought to faith in the Lord Jesus Christ through Knox's preaching and came to visit John one night to see how he was.

'A friend indeed,' John thought to himself, as he served his friend a warm glass of ale.

'Show me that letter they're all talking about,' Spens asked. 'I need to know if they really have any case against you.'

Knox trusted this man. He wasn't a fair weather Christian – and he knew the law.

After a few moments Spens laid the letter down on a side table and smiled. 'Well, that's a relief. I was concerned that this charge of treason would stick, but I can see that they have nothing against you. They will still accuse you, but I know that God will be your help ... and if there is anything I can do, John, just ask.'

After Spens sneaked out into the darkness, John went upstairs to check on his two young sons, asleep in their bed. 'There is nothing I would do or say differently to what I have done and said,' he muttered. 'But treason ... I must face the reality of this and make plans for my boys. It is good that Marjorie's mother is now in England. I should send the boys to her care after Christmas.'

The summons, however, came before Christmas and the news spread across the whole city. As Knox made his way into the inner court, all the outer chambers were filled to the gunnels with members of John's faithful congregation. For once they outnumbered his enemies.

As John walked into the chamber room, a sudden hush descended on the nobles and courtiers present. Earls and lords sat on their chairs facing John. Spens smiled gently to him from his seat amongst them. 'At least there is one I can call friend,' John sighed. Then from a side chamber the call came, 'The Queen!'

All rose and bowed as Her Splendid Majesty Mary Queen of Scots entered, all jewels and necklaces, to take her place at the head of the council table. At her right hand was Master Maxwell. John hadn't realised how high this man had climbed in the court. To be at the right hand side of the queen was quite an achievement for someone who had fought courageously against the queen's mother in times past.

Mary looked at John as he stood at the other end of the table. She smiled slyly before bursting into giggles. Maxwell returned the queen's smile and joined in with her private joke before reading the charges that John was accused of.

'The Queen's Majesty is informed that you have raised a riot against her. We present the evidence here – a letter signed by yourself. You have been summoned before Her Majesty and the nobility so that they may witness the accusations made against you and the evidence that the queen presents.'

The letter was passed around the noblemen and Knox acknowledged that the handwriting was indeed his. The queen ordered Knox to read his letter aloud to the court, which he did.

In the letter he had written to other believers to remind them of how God had comforted and cared for them in the past, but how now, because believers were neglecting the true church, false teaching and heresy was once more gaining a foothold. 'The holy sacraments are abused; Masses are openly said and maintained; the blood of some of our dearest ministers has been shed without fear of punishment.'

Knox urged the believers to come to the support of the church; he pleaded with them in his letter to come to Edinburgh in order to preserve the 'Kirk'. 'It may be that you have been persuaded not to come; perhaps you think it is unnecessary or that it will offend the powers of the land; but my good hope is that neither flattery nor fear shall make you retreat from Jesus Christ.'

With that, John placed the letter back down on the table. The queen's advocate, the same Spens who had visited with Knox not so long ago, stood up to read out the accusation against him.

With this done, the queen turned to the noblemen present and haughtily announced, 'Have you ever heard, my lords, a more despiteful and treasonable letter. Master Knox, are you not deeply sorry and repent that any such letter has passed your pen?'

Knox demanded to know what his offence was. One of the noblemen replied, 'You have encouraged the people to be gathered together ....'

'But this has been done before,' John complained, 'no charge was brought then.'

'That was then, this is now,' replied Maxwell. 'We have no need of such meetings as we once had.'

The debate continued until the queen angrily interrupted the proceedings. 'You're just trifling with him. Who gave him the authority to gather my people together? Is that not treason?'

One man, Lord Ruthven, stood up to respond, 'No, my lady. Knox gathers the people together to hear prayer and sermons almost daily and whatever Your Grace or others will think of it, we do not think that it is treason.'

'Hold your peace!' Mary snapped. 'Let him answer for himself.'

Knox then went on to argue that not all public gatherings were unlawful and that he had never gathered more than four people together in Scotland by his own will. 'It has only been under the instruction of other believers that I have preached to these great crowds. What I have done, I have done at the commandment of the Kirk of this realm and therefore I think I have done no wrong.'

Knox then drew the queen's attention to the fact that it was the wish of many Roman Catholics to exterminate the Protestants and their church. Mary began to get more than a bit annoyed.

'You're not in the pulpit now,' she complained.

'I am in the place where I am demanded of conscience to speak the truth: and therefore I speak,' Knox retorted.

After further discussion, Knox was allowed to return to his house for the night while the council made their final deliberations before voting on the outcome of the case. The verdict was unanimous.

'Not Guilty!' – a messenger ran up to the front door of Knox's house the following morning, knocking violently on the door. 'Not Guilty, Master Knox – the vote was unanimous – you're free of all charges!'

The messenger might have expected a more joyous response from Knox when he heard the news ... but Knox simply patted the youngster on the head and went back to his studies. The fact that so many men had turned against him made him feel more lonely than he had ever felt before.

Later on, when the leaders of the Kirk met together for their assembly, Knox said nothing during any of the debates – he was completely silent until at the very end he rose to address the meeting. 'Beloved Brethren, in recent days I have been accused of being a seditious man, one that uses and abuses power. But it has been by the appointment of this very assembly, that I have been given power to gather the brethren together and to warn them of dangers as well as to teach them from the Word of God. If the Kirk do not either absolve me or condemn me, then I shall never, in public or in private, as a public minister, open my mouth in doctrine or in reasoning.'

With that, John withdrew from the assembly and the remaining men discussed the issue of his guilt or innocence. After much deliberation the Kirk vindicated him, saying that he had only been about his duty.

But the wounds still hurt ... several of the men who had stood in judgement over him in the court would never speak to Knox again.

As the months and years went on, the plots to overthrow Knox and the democratic Kirk of Scotland increased. The queen's court ignored the Kirk's right of liberty. Again, the main complaint that the court had against the Kirk was John Knox. The court wanted the Kirk to thank the queen for tolerating them so graciously. So a small gathering of court and Kirk officials met together one day to discuss the demands of the queen and the doctrine of Knox.

'Knox declares that subjects are at liberty to disobey their monarchs if they think them unjust. Surely not?' one lord announced.

At this point, Knox himself decided to speak. 'God craves not only that a man do no iniquity in his own person, but also that he oppose himself to all iniquity as far as in him lies.'

'Would you have subjects controlling their leaders?' one courtier gasped out loud.

'There is no harm,' Knox retorted, 'to have ignorant leaders moderated by the wisdom and discretion of godly subjects. To resist a tyrant is not to resist God.'

Knox's words fell on deaf ears ... and too late the people of Scotland realised that he had been right about their pretty young queen all along.

Scandal, Scandal, Scandal!

A tall nobleman had caught Queen Mary's eye, a Lord Darnley, who soon became her lover and her king. She made him Earl of Ross, then Duke of Rothesay. She married him without the court's permission. She even gave him a crown of his own. The men who had listened to the accusations of treason against Knox, who had given the queen whatever she wanted, now were accused of being rebels and denounced by the queen they had so favoured.

The people flocked to St Giles once more where Knox, in the presence of the congregation and Lord Darnley, preached a sermon on the theme of power and responsibility. John declared how wicked princes were a plague sent to sinful people. Needless to say, Darnley returned home in a fury.

Knox, however, cared not for the thoughts or actions of others who reacted against the truthful teaching of God's Word. He had a home to return to and a warm welcome from a young wife and a new baby girl, for over a year ago he had married a woman named Margaret Stewart. She was well connected, as she had in her veins royal blood. This match had infuriated Queen Mary, as she couldn't bare to see Knox so well married.

Knox didn't give two hoots that the queen was annoyed with him for marrying into nobility. He didn't care what anybody thought of a low-ranking preacher marrying a distant relative of the queen.

Knox's two boys now lived permanently with their grandmother in England ... where Knox would regularly visit them. 'It is perhaps a safer place for young men to grow into adulthood,' he had explained to Mrs Bowes. 'Queen Elizabeth has given me safe passage to travel here. It is a Protestant land under a Protestant queen. Whereas Scotland ...' he dropped off mid-sentence. The situation in Scotland was not so encouraging.

Rumours were rife about the queen. Scandal and intrigue surrounded the crown. The talk in the towns was all about the young queen's supposed relationship with the musician Rizzio. 'She's not been married that long to Darnley and now here she is cavorting with another man,' a fishwife told her friend as they talked over the fence.

'They say she is with child, and some question who the father is,' was the reply.

Some weeks later the talk was of a far more violent nature, 'Did you hear that the queen's favourite, Rizzio, was murdered by the king in the palace grounds ... that's the rumour.'

'Aye, and it's more than a rumour. There's people who say that the king's dagger was still in the body as Rizzio was flung down the stairs.'

'Well,' the gossip replied, 'Those that live by the sword, die by the sword.'

And that was very true.

Darnley had allowed his temper and evil heart to gain the upper hand. He had never been a brave warrior but it was very likely that he had been the instigator of Rizzio's murder. However, not too long after he stuck his dagger in the side of his wife's favourite courtier, he suffered a violent death himself. The rumours began to circulate again.

'The king is dead, but the queen doesn't look that sorry about it,' was another whisper over the fence.

'She didn't even give him a proper funeral, can you believe it?' the friend replied.

'At least she got that child of hers baptized before her husband was strangled. There is an heir to the throne which is a relief .... '

'But to be strangled. Ugghh ... what a dreadful way to die and then whoever did it tried to cover it up with that explosion!'

'It's hard to believe we're talking about royalty here and not barbarians!'

'Some would say there is little difference these days,' and the conversation was over.

But that wasn't the end of the royal scandal ... no sooner had she despatched one husband than rumours that Mary had taken another lover were soon circling the city. The Earl of Bothwell was now her new favourite. Many of the reformers remembered how he had once been their enemy. He had skilfully survived and prospered throughout the many shifts and changes in Scotland – because the only cause that he really supported was himself.

He'd supported Mary de Guise and had been a central player in the arrest of George Wishart. Now he was Mary's favourite and was almost untouchable.

He had soldiers and ruffians under his command and the queen was handing him gifts of land and titles as though they were children's treats. Everything that stood in the way of his power was removed – even his wife. A quick divorce meant Mary soon announced her plans to marry Bothwell and twelve days later they were indeed man and wife; in fact it was only three months after the death of her husband, Darnley.

This marriage wasn't popular with Roman Catholics or Protestants. Mary's catastrophic life spiralled further into disgrace and dishonour. Her unwise passion for the Earl of Bothwell showed her people just the sort of woman they had to rule over them ... she wasn't wise, she certainly wasn't discrete, was she even moral?

And as Mary's life descended into scandal, Scotland descended into disunity. The lords who had once flattered her, now fought her – with good reason. Bothwell took up his sword – perhaps to protect his queen and wife, but more likely to protect his own interests. Mary, foolishly passionate as ever, rode to his defence, but she was captured. Her Lord Bothwell did not behave so gallantly as she had. She had ridden to his defence, but he rode to his own freedom, heading for the hills while the Queen of Scotland was marched back to her capital city in disgrace.

Where she had once been cheered as a rare beauty, she was now jeered. Dishevelled and dressed in borrowed or stolen garments – she was a laughing stock. She in the past had taken great delight in belittling John Knox. Now her captors had to protect her from the mob who would have cheerfully torn her to pieces in the city.

Knox and others were gathered together to sign articles and other laws to protect the Church of Scotland. Mary was eventually persuaded to abdicate the throne to her young son.

Of course a young infant cannot rule – so once more a Regent had to be found. James Stewart, Queen Mary's half-brother, held the reigns of power in the meantime. A nobleman and a Protestant, he was a strong pair of hands to lead the country, Knox thought as the young infant prince was crowned in Stirling, under the watchful gaze of his uncle.

Imprisoned in Loch Leven Castle, it was the beginning of the end for Mary Queen of Scots. Calls were made for the deposed queen to be brought to trial for her actions and if necessary to be put to death. Knox felt that there would be no lasting peace in the country until that took place, but with the help of a young page, Mary got hold of the keys to her cell and soon was on a horse bound for the west.

Then after another defeat, Mary fled for England – and there ends her sorry tale. Nineteen years in prison, then death under an executioner's sword, killed at the command of her cousin.

Strong and Sure

Knox could hardly believe the news he had just heard. He solemnly shook his greying head. The Regent had been killed. The news John had received that morning simply proved to him how fragile and unstable the nation of Scotland was. An assassin had shot James Stewart and the country was in turmoil once again.

Knox was still under attack by Queen Mary's supporters, many of whom had not left the capital. Knox was accused of murder, witchcraft, and immorality. Each accusation was firmly squashed by Knox himself. He had the appearance of an elderly man, with his grey hair and walking stick – but his mind was the sharpest on the Royal Mile.

His body was stooped and his face haggard but his passion for the truth was undiminished. Despite having suffered from a stroke he still preached fearlessly and with clarity.

This kind of preaching, as always, put him in great danger. One day, a musket was fired through the window of his study. The bullet went straight through the back of the chair that Knox normally sat in.

A servant brushed up some of the debris as she exclaimed, 'Master Knox, if you had been sitting in this chair, as is your custom, it would be you being swept up from this carpet and not bits of that chandelier.'

Knox snorted rather gruffly before turning to his young wife, who was holding another baby girl in her arms. They had three little lassies now. 'I've been advised to leave for St Andrews,' he told her.

'It's maybe a wise decision, my dear,' his wife agreed. 'Every week you're falsely accused or receive a threat of some kind or other. It won't take us long to prepare for the journey .... Do you want to go?'

John looked out of the broken window and sighed. Something in him wanted to return to St Andrews, the place where he had first heard the call to preach. It would be good to go back, to get away from the spite, the lies, the fears for his young family.

On the table by his side, were the first few paragraphs of a piece of writing he was putting together in support of the new Church of Scotland. 'Our Kirk is not bound to any one place, but is dispersed upon the face of the whole earth; having one God, one faith, one baptism and one Lord Jesus, Saviour of all that truly believe.'

Soon the Knox family left for St Andrews. They hadn't been long in the city when it was evident that Knox's health was in decline.

Knox realised that his body was getting weaker by the day, and that his time on earth was short, 'Be merciful unto me, O Lord ... after many battles, I find nothing in me but vanity and corruption. For, in quietness I am negligent, in trouble impatient ... and I am carried away with vain fantasies that alas, O Lord, withdraw me from the presence of thy Majesty. Pride and ambition assault me on the one part, covetousness and malice trouble me on the other ....'

But even in his frailty he still preached and taught. Some commented on the fact that when he climbed into the pulpit he would have to lean against it for the strength to stay upright, but by the end of the sermon his energy and vigour were such that he could have flown out of it if he had wished.

However, moments after leaving the church, if you had met him on his walk home you would have said you had met a weak and frail old man, holding a staff in one hand and being held up by a servant with the other.

'It was here that we first caught the reek of Patrick Hamilton,' John whispered to his servant as they walked slowly home one day from the service. 'And it was here in the St Andrew's bottle dungeon that my good friend George Wishart was imprisoned before his death.'

The servant didn't reply. Unless he was preaching God's Word, Knox's voice was so feeble you could barely hear what he had to say.

Returning to his lodgings, his young wife looked on concerned at his rapidly weakening body. 'I don't think I will go out anymore today,' he muttered.

The weeks following, Knox didn't leave the house unless it was to preach. His students and other young men came to listen to him at his home. Some would later look back on these days as great days – ones that made them follow a true path, the path of faith and salvation.

Barely a year after his arrival at St Andrews, the political situation changed once more and the unrest that had scourged the capital city of Edinburgh turned into a relative peace. Soon there was a letter in Knox's hands, once more pleading with him to return to preach in Edinburgh.

'You're too weak to go,' his wife complained.

'Weak or not I will go – but only if they give me the freedom to speak freely.'

That freedom was given and in 1572 John Knox returned to the church of St Giles. While he was there, news arrived in the city of the massacre of French Protestants that took place on St Bartholemew's Eve. Men, women and children were slaughtered in the streets, for which the Pope in Rome offered up a special service of thanksgiving.

Knox could see where things were going. He knew the dangers that faced the church and the weakness of his own body and health. He made it his purpose to ensure that the church of St Giles was left in good hands. In November of that year, a new minister was appointed to the congregation; one for which John praised God. 'May the Lord bless him a thousand-fold above what I had, if it is his pleasure.'

Two days after this new appointment, John Knox began a cough – a signal that his already weakening health was becoming worse.

Knox took heed of this signal and began to put things in order – paying bills, sending messages to friends and enemies. Some men who had long ignored him or worse, were sent heartfelt notes from the pen of the frail old man. He still hoped that some of them would repent of their sin and turn to Christ.

As the month of December drew near, John even instructed someone to order his coffin. His final hours were filled with prayers – 'Live in Christ! Lord, grant true pastors to thy Kirk!'

His final request was to his young wife to read to him from John chapter 17.

> *These words spake Jesus and lifted up his eyes to heaven and said: Father, the hour is come: glorify thy son, that thy son also may glorify thee.*
>
> *As thou hast given him power over all flesh, that he should give eternal life to as many as thou hast given him.*
>
> *And this is eternal life, that they might know thee, the only true God, and Jesus Christ whom thou has sent.*

John Knox was buried in the churchyard behind St Giles. It was said at his grave, 'Here lies one who never feared the face of man.'

He never feared the face of man or woman, nobleman, king or queen. He spoke the truth and didn't flinch. In the battles ahead, and there were many for the Kirk, others spoke the same truth who had been inspired by his fearless faith.

In fact, his own daughter, one of the three little lassies he left behind had more than her share of her father's grit – standing up to the King of England himself to protect her preacher husband, John Welch.

Lawson, John Knox's successor continued to fight for 'the Crown rights of the redeemer'.

Another man, Melville, told the king to his face, 'There are two kings and two kingdoms in Scotland – there is James Stewart and his kingdom and there is Jesus Christ and his kingdom – the Kirk ... whose subject James VI is – and not a lord nor a head but a member.'

Welch, Lawson and Melville all died in exile, John Knox's little lass was the only one ever to return to Scotland.

Today you would be hard pushed to find Knox's Scotland ... the one he fought and prayed for.

His legacy stands in the freedoms we are blessed with ... but he is still being falsely accused by ignorant people.

May God bless the land of John Knox and the Church of God with the strength and conviction to fight for the truth, for the Word of God and for the Sovereignty of Christ.

Take up the Sword. It's not just Knox's sword – it's yours: The Sword of the Spirit – the Word of God. Take it, believe it and use it.

Thinking Further Topics

1. John Knox the Bodyguard

Was it a surprise to you to read that John Knox was a bodyguard? He is famous for being a preacher, why do you think people are surprised to hear that he was once a bodyguard and good with a sword?

2. John Knox the Tutor

It is said of John Knox that he was a very good tutor and knew how to get the best out of his students. What can you see of the character and practice of John Knox that would make him a good tutor?

3. John Knox the Friend

George Wishart was a friend and mentor to John Knox. Wishart was a great influence on him. What similarities can you see between George and John? After George's death, in what ways did John become more like George?

4. John Knox the Freedom Fighter

Today, we are used to having freedoms, but in Knox's day it was a different story. What freedoms do we have today that people in the 1500s didn't? Do you agree that people in power always deserve power? Who gives them that power in the first place? Can you remember any of the things that John Knox said about rulers and how subjects should behave towards them? What should we do today when governments go against the Word of God? Knox believed that you could support violent resistance, if you were resisting godless rulers. Are there times when we should resist violence and obey political powers – even though those powers do not obey God?

5. John Knox the Galley Slave

Life was tough on board the galley-ship. John Knox was a captive and a slave. Name some of the hardships he had to face. How did John get into trouble with the ship's captain, earning him a beating? However, John didn't care for his sore back – what did he care for most of all?

6. John Knox the Preacher

John preached in several places and to many people. Name some places where he preached. Though John hadn't wanted to be a preacher at first, he eventually changed his mind. Why do you think that was? What difficulties did John face as he preached the truth?

7. John Knox the Writer

John Knox wrote many books and sermons. Perhaps his most famous piece is the one he wrote against female monarchs. Because of this, many people today accuse him of being against women. Why is this not true? In what way was this article something that needed to be written? What should women, and indeed men, be thankful to John Knox for today?

John Knox Timeline

1510   Pocket watch invented by Peter Henlein.

1512   Michelangelo completes Sistine Chapel
        frescoes.

1514   John Knox born (possible date).

1516   Erasmus publishes Greek New Testament.

1517   Luther posts 95 Theses.

1525   Tyndale publishes English New Testament.

1536   Knox graduates from University of
        St Andrews and is ordained as a priest.
        Calvin publishes *Institutes of the Christian
        Religion*.

1540   Knox begins his legal career while also
        working as a tutor.

1545   Knox becomes bodyguard to George Wishart.

1546   Wishart martyred; Cardinal Beaton.
        murdered; St Andrews Castle under siege.

1547   Knox preaches his first sermon; Knox
        imprisoned as galley slave.

1549   Knox becomes the pastor of a church in
        Berwick, England.

1550   Knox meets Marjorie Bowes and her mother.

1553   Mary Tudor becomes queen.

1554   Knox flees to France, then Geneva. Knox
        leaves for Frankfurt.

1555   Returns to Geneva, then Scotland.

1556   Returns to Geneva again with his wife,
        Marjorie, and mother-in-law.

1558   Knox writes *The First Blast of the Trumpet
Against the Monstrous Regiment of Women*.
Elizabeth I becomes Queen of England.

1559   Knox returns to Scotland.

1560   Knox's wife dies.

1561   Knox helps write *First Book of Discipline*;
Mary Queen of Scots returns.

1564   Knox marries for a second time.

1566   Knox writes *History of the Reformation of
Religion in Scotland*.

1572   St Bartholomew's Day Massacre in France.
John Knox dies.

1578   James VI takes over government in Scotland.

1581   Francis Drake returns to England after
circumnavigating the globe.

1587   Mary Stuart executed.
Sir Walter Raleigh founds the first English
Colony in North America (North Carolina).

1592   Presbyterianism becomes the established
form of church government in Scotland by
Act of Parliament.

Note from the Author: Catherine Mackenzie

I've loved books from as far back as I can remember. As a child, my parents offered me a new book if I would agree to take my medicine without any fuss. Believe it or not I agreed to do that – which goes to show how much I liked books.

I like all sorts of books – but over time I would say that true stories have always been the ones to make me sit up and take notice. History is definitely more amazing and off the wall than fiction – because it is true.

That's why I've ended up writing these kinds of stories – real life adventures about real people who worshipped the one, true, real God.

My own story is not one that I would pick up a pen and write about ... but God has given me a story anyway ... a story that's all about him and what he has done in my life. He sent his Son to save sinners – that includes me. His Son suffered on the cross, taking sin on his sinless self – he did this for me. He rose again from the dead so that his people can have eternal life. I am thankful that I am among that number ... a group of sinners, saved by grace, that includes Richard Wurmbrand, Billy Graham, Mary Slessor, John Knox and many many others. So many – how will we ever be able to write about all of them?

TRAILBLAZER SERIES

Gladys Aylward, No Mountain too High
ISBN 978-1-85792-594-4
Corrie ten Boom, The Watchmaker's Daughter
ISBN 978-1-85792-116-8
David Brainerd, A Love for the Lost
ISBN 978-1-84550-695-7
Paul Brand, The Shoes that Love Made
ISBN 978-1-84550-630-8
Billy Bray, Saved from the Deepest Pit
ISBN 978-1-84550-788-6
Bill Bright, Dare to be Different
ISBN 978-1-85792-945-4
John Bunyan, The Journey of a Pilgrim
ISBN 978-1-84550-458-8
Amy Carmichael, Rescuer by Night
ISBN 978-1-85792-946-1
John Calvin, After Darkness Light
ISBN 978-1-84550-084-9
Jonathan Edwards, America's Genius
ISBN 978-1-84550-329-1
Michael Faraday, Spiritual Dynamo
ISBN 978-1-84550-156-3
Billy Graham, Just Get Up Out Of Your Seat
ISBN 978-1-84550-095-5
Adoniram Judson, Danger on the Streets of Gold
ISBN 978-1-85792-660-6
Isobel Kuhn, Lights in Lisuland
ISBN 978-1-85792-610-1
C.S. Lewis, The Storyteller
ISBN 978-1-85792-487-9
Eric Liddell, Finish the Race
ISBN 978-1-84550-590-5

Start collecting this series now!

Ten Boys who used their Talents:
ISBN 978-1-84550-146-4
Paul Brand, Ghillean Prance, C.S.Lewis,
C.T. Studd, Wilfred Grenfell, J.S. Bach,
James Clerk Maxwell, Samuel Morse,
George Washington Carver, John Bunyan.

Ten Girls who used their Talents:
ISBN 978-1-84550-147-1
Helen Roseveare, Maureen McKenna,
Anne Lawson, Harriet Beecher Stowe,
Sarah Edwards, Selina Countess of Huntingdon,
Mildred Cable, Katie Ann MacKinnon,
Patricia St. John, Mary Verghese.

Ten Boys who Changed the World:
ISBN 978-1-85792-579-1
David Livingstone, Billy Graham, Brother Andrew,
John Newton, William Carey, George Müller,
Nicky Cruz, Eric Liddell, Luis Palau,
Adoniram Judson.

Ten Girls who Changed the World:
ISBN 978-1-85792-649-1
Corrie Ten Boom, Mary Slessor,
Joni Eareckson Tada, Isobel Kuhn,
Amy Carmichael, Elizabeth Fry, Evelyn Brand,
Gladys Aylward, Catherine Booth, Jackie Pullinger.

Ten Boys who Made a Difference:
ISBN 978-1-85792-775-7
Augustine of Hippo, Jan Hus, Martin Luther,
Ulrich Zwingli, William Tyndale, Hugh Latimer,
John Calvin, John Knox, Lord Shaftesbury,
Thomas Chalmers.

Ten Girls who Made a Difference:
ISBN 978-1-85792-776-4
Monica of Thagaste, Catherine Luther,
Susanna Wesley, Ann Judson, Maria Taylor,
Susannah Spurgeon, Bethan Lloyd-Jones,
Edith Schaeffer, Sabina Wurmbrand,
Ruth Bell Graham.

Ten Boys who Made History:
ISBN 978-1-85792-836-5
Charles Spurgeon, Jonathan Edwards,
Samuel Rutherford, D L Moody,
Martin Lloyd Jones, A W Tozer, John Owen, Robert Murray McCheyne, Billy Sunday,
George Whitfield.

Ten Girls who Made History:
ISBN 978-1-85792-837-2
Ida Scudder, Betty Green, Jeanette Li,
Mary Jane Kinnaird, Bessie Adams,
Emma Dryer, Lottie Moon, Florence Nightingale,
Henrietta Mears, Elisabeth Elliot.

Ten Boys who Didn't Give In:
ISBN 978-1-84550-035-1
Polycarp, Alban, Sir John Oldcastle
Thomas Cramer, George Wishart,
James Chalmers, Dietrich Bonhoeffer,
Nate Saint, Ivan Moiseyev,
Graham Staines.

Ten Girls who Didn't Give In:
ISBN 978-1-84550-036-8
Blandina, Perpetua, Lady Jane Grey,
Anne Askew, Lysken Dirks, Marion Harvey,
Margaret Wilson, Judith Weinberg,
Betty Stam, Esther John.

CHRISTIAN FOCUS PUBLICATIONS

Christian Focus | Christian Heritage | CF4K | Mentor

Christian Focus Publications publishes books for adults and children under its four main imprints: Christian Focus, CF4K, Mentor and Christian Heritage. Our books reflect our conviction that God's Word is reliable and Jesus is the way to know him, and live for ever with him.

Our children's publication list includes a Sunday School curriculum that covers pre-school to early teens, and puzzle and activity books. We also publish personal and family devotional titles, biographies and inspirational stories that children will love.

If you are looking for quality Bible teaching for children then we have an excellent range of Bible stories and age-specific theological books.

From pre-school board books to teenage apologetics, we have it covered!

Find us at our web page:
www.christianfocus.com

CF4•K
Because you're never too young to know Jesus